D1396624

THE UNOFFICIAL HARRY POTTER GUIDEBOOK

Spells - Potions - Characters - Magical Places - Trivia & More in the Wizarding World

Ken Shaw

CONTENTS

HOW TO USE THE BOOK?

The book is conveniently sorted into sections with characters description, facts, spells, potions, quizzes and other interesting trivia, so you can go to any section you are interested in any order.

But I would still recommend reading the book sequentially to refresh your memory before the quiz.

<u>Thank You for Purchasing & Reading!</u>

I hope you find this book useful and fun.

MAGIC

- So this ... this magic is what I can do?

— What exactly do you know how to do?

"Different things," Riddle breathed. A blush suffused his face, starting from his neck and rising to his sunken cheeks. He was in a fever. - I can move things without touching them. I can make animals do what I want, without any training. If someone makes me angry, I can make something bad happen to him. I can hurt a person if I want to.

- Young Tom Riddle tells Dumbledore about his magical skills

Magic is an ability that allows you to control objects and phenomena with the help of internal (mainly psychic) energy. Magic is morally and ethically neutral.

Magic is a supernatural force that can change the fabric of reality on a fundamental level. The ability to use magic is an inherited trait and is passed down to descendants from ancestors, which allows witches and sorcerers to practice magic.

The basic properties of magic are quite simple — even a two-year-old child can use some of its forms, which in children manifest themselves in spontaneous magical outbursts, usually when experiencing strong emotions or fear. In the first book, Neville Longbottom told about the first manifestation of his magic at the age of eight. But most often, the first manifestations of magical abilities occur at 6-7 years. The inherent power and huge potential of magic is very tempting for young inexperienced minds and can lead to various abuses. It is enough to recall the young Tom Riddle. For this reason, promising young witches and wizards at the age of 11 go to Hogwarts or other magical schools to study their abilities, learn the art of controlling their own magic and realize the depth of personal responsibility for its misuse.

Magic is not available to Muggles and Squibs, which distinguishes them from wizards. This restriction forces them to use various technical devices and develop science and technology. In the same sense, many wizards are not able to use most Muggle devices and do not know the basic principles of their work. For example, completely ordinary concepts for Muggles like electricity or electronics cause them deep bewilderment and misunderstanding. Both Muggles and wizards see their own possibilities as completely ordinary and completely logical, although if they were closely acquainted with the alternative, they would find it amusing, exciting and even mysterious.

In accordance with the International Statute of Secrecy, adopted in 1689, wizards must hide their magical abilities from the ordinary world, so most Muggles are completely unaware of the existence of the wizarding world. Being declassified in the Muggle world, magic could be considered the fourth major branch of science, alongside chemistry, biology, and physics. However, the main direction of modern Muggle science is the study of the natural physical laws of the surrounding world, and due to its supernaturalness, magic is not. It is difficult to even imagine what would have happened in such a case because the postulates of modern science seem to be inviolable to many Muggles.

Dark magic is the prerogative of evil forces. Being carried away by the dark arts, many wizards finally lose their humanity and become real criminals. That is why many areas of magical science are prohibited in the magical world, and for their use, you can depart in Azkaban.

Magic Of People

In humans, the ability or inability to create magic is determined by genetic inheritance. It is normal for a couple of wizards to have magic in their children, but this phenomenon is quite rare in a married couple of Muggles. This is because the magic gene present in the DNA of witches and sorcerers is dominant. Squibs are people who were born into magical families but can't do magic. This happens when the descendant of wizards does not manifest such a gene for some reason, as a result of which he becomes incapable of wizardry.

A witch or wizard born to Muggle parents is known as a Muggle-born. This happens when a Muggle family descends from a squib, whose descendants suddenly have the magic gene active many generations later. There are many more Muggle-born wizards than squibs, but this may be due to the disparate scale of the populations of the world of ordinary people and the world of magic.

For the direct realization of their vital magical desires, magicians use spells.

More complex magical actions are performed with the help of magical rituals. One of these rituals was used by Lord Voldemort for his rebirth.

Magic rites can include one or more complex spells, which, unlike ordinary spells, are not limited to one phrase and one wave of the wand. One of these rites, for example, is the spell "The Trace" — that is imposed on underage wizards.

The Magic Of Intelligent Magical Creatures

Wizards, who, for the most part, consider themselves the pinnacle of evolution, are prejudiced against other magical races and, in their pride, refer them to intelligent beings or even to animals endowed with only glimpses of reason. Meanwhile, the magic of intelligent magical creatures is in many cases inaccessible to wizards. Magicians refer to intelligent magical creatures as vampires, veela, giants, goblins, house-elfs, centaurs, werewolfs, merpeople and sphinxes. Also, trolls and acromantulas can probably be attributed to them.

- **Magic of veela**. In addition to the ability to conjure, inherent in witches, veela have the art of charming men. Very few of them can resist these charms, especially if veela wants it. In a state of anger or at will, veela can turn into something very similar to a harpy. A sharp-billed bird's head, scaly wings and the ability to throw fire are the hallmarks of veela in this state.

- **Magic of goblins**. This manifests itself mainly in the ability to process metals in a special way. Items made by goblins are often distinguished by outstanding magical properties.

- **Magic of house-elfs**. This manifests itself in the ability of house-elfs to witchcraft without a magic wand (elves can be used both household and not too traumatic combat spells). Also, elfs can ignore some enchantments (they can apparition in places protected by anti-disapparition jinx).

- **Magic of giants**. This manifests itself mainly in the immunity of giants to certain types of magic and potions.

- **Magic of vampires**. Little is known about the magic of the vampires. Children can be born from the union of a vampire and a wizard, and such facts are known. Perhaps such children have full-fledged magical abilities. Nothing is known about the vampires' abilities to move in the shadows, possessing supernatural powers, and transforming into bats :)

- **Magic of centaurs**. This is quite weak, but they are perfectly versed in such magical science as Divination, in particular, in Astrology (divination by the movement of the heavenly bodies), although their ideas about this discipline are somewhat different from human ones. Since 1996, the centaur Firenze, who is perfectly familiar with the most diverse types of centaurs divination, which people sometimes do not even guess about, has been teaching at Hogwarts.

Magic Items

When magic is invested in an object of the material world, it acquires new properties, sometimes completely unimaginable. Magic is a rather dangerous thing, and its thoughtless use can lead to very unpleasant consequences. After all, it is possible to change not only the structure of space but also time itself; that is, to change the fundamental laws of the universe. Such dangerous magical inventions include, for example, Time-Turner.

Sometimes, magical energy is placed in a certain object, which begins to have unusual abilities or even reasonable behavior, such as, for example, Voldemort's horcruxes. Items containing powerful, dark, magical energy are called dark artifacts. However, there are light magic and neutral artifacts, such as Sorting Hat or Portkey.

The magical energy contained in an object can eventually scatter, or vice versa, gain strength (usually, this applies to dark magic and all sorts of dark curses).

You can enchant both things made from inorganic materials (magic items) and from organic materials (for example, magic sweets).

Potions

Wizards and witches prepare potions, putting their magic into them. Without magic, potions will not work.

Magical Creatures And Plants

Obviously, psychic energy is more or less inherent, not only in people but, in general, in all living beings on the planet. Therefore, some animals and plants that concentrate this energy in sufficient quantities may have certain supernatural properties.

This can manifest itself both in the appearance of magical creatures and plants (the same dragons, centaurs and others) and in the abilities of individuals, outwardly indistinguishable from their non-magical counterparts.

WIZARDING SCHOOLS

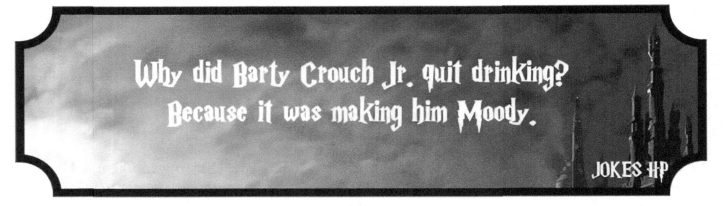

Why did Barty Crouch Jr. quit drinking?
Because it was making him Moody.

JOKES HP

Wizarding schools are educational institutions in which young wizards are taught the art of magic: Charms, potions and other magical sciences.

The number of countries that have their own magic schools is negligible, compared to the number of those that do not have them. This is because the magical population of most countries prefers home schooling. Also, sometimes the magic community of a particular country can be tiny or sparse over a large territory, and, in this case, they consider correspondence courses the most economical way to teach young people.

In total, there are eleven ancient and prestigious schools of magic in the world, each of which is registered in the International Confederation of Wizards. Mostly, they are boarding schools where students of different ages and nationalities receive education and live for several years.

Small pedagogical institutions that are not under such proper control, as they come and go are difficult to track, and they are rarely registered by the relevant Ministry of Magic (in this case, you can not vouch for the educational standard that they can offer). Anyone who wants to find out if there is an approved magic school in their region should send an owl with a request to the Educational Department of the International Confederation of Wizards.

The exact location of each of those eleven schools is kept strictly secret. Schools are not only afraid of Muggle persecution, because there is a sad fact that at various times in their long history, all these institutions have suffered from the influence of magical wars and hostile attention from both foreign and domestic magical communities (not only in the UK, where the education of magical youth has become the subject of ministerial intervention and pressure). As a rule, magic schools are located in landlocked territories in mountainous areas (although there are notable exceptions), since such regions are difficult for Muggles to reach and are easier to defend against Dark Wizards.

The existence of several schools is due to territorial, linguistic and social differences, as in

Beauxbatons children from Romanesque Europe study, in Durmstrang - most likely from Slavic, Scandinavian and some German-speaking countries, and in Hogwarts - residents of the British Isles.

It is known that more students study at Durmstrang and Beauxbatons than at Hogwarts.

Famous Wizarding Schools

1. Hogwarts School of Witchcraft and Wizardry (United Kingdom)

2. Beauxbatons Academy of Magic (France)

3. Durmstrang Institute (Northern Europe)

4. Koldovstoretz (Russia)

5. Mahoutokoro (Japan)

6. Uagadou School of Magic (Uganda)

7. Castelobruxo (Brazil)

8. Ilvermorny School of Witchcraft and Wizardry (USA)

Competitions Between Schools

1. Triwizard Tournament

2. Wizarding Schools Potions Championship

Slytherin, Founder Of Salazar Slytherin

1. Notable Deans: Severus Snape, Horace Slughorn

2. Colors: Green, Silver

3. Qualities of students: Cunning, determination, ambition, resourcefulness, thirst for power.

4. A ghost: Bloody Baron

5. The symbol is a beast: Snake

6. Element: Water

7. Magic item associated with the name of the founder of the house: Slytherin's Locket

8. The enchanted place associated with the name of the founder of the house: Chamber of Secrets

9. Magical animal associated with the name of the founder of the house: Serpent of Slytherin

10. The Slytherin Lounge: A low, long dungeon with walls of wild stone, an elaborately carved fireplace, and greenish lamps hanging from the ceiling on chains. The entrance is through a bare wall in one of the underground corridors. When you name the password, part of the wall goes to the side.

11. Some characteristic features: opposition to the rest of the faculties (at Quidditch matches, fans of Gryffindor, Ravenclaw and Hufflepuff unite, no matter which house plays against Slytherin). Disregard for school rules (as Dumbledore tells Harry Potter in the book "Harry Potter and the Chamber of Secrets"). Increased attention to their own health and physical fitness (Slytherins often surpass Gryffindors and other students in strength and height).

MAGICAL PLACES

Unlike such fairy-tale and fantasy sagas as the Lord of the Rings, where the action refers to the forgotten, mythological times of the history of the world, or the "Chronicles of Narnia", localized in a parallel world connected to the earthly world by magic portals, the events of the Harry Potter series of novels take place on the Earth modern to the author. Magical places, such as Diagon Alley, Platform 9¾, Hogwarts, are not located in a different space-time continuum but are simply separated from the surrounding world by enchantments that make them impenetrable to Muggles.

These are the explanations about Hogwarts given by Hermione Granger to Harry Potter during the Quidditch World Cup in the book "Harry Potter and the Goblet of Fire."Numerous evidence of the absence of a sharp boundary between magical and non-magical places in the world of Harry Potter can be found in the events of the Seven Books themselves.

Next, we will talk about these interesting places... in which there were actions that affected the universe of Harry Potter.

Please do not forget to leave reviews about the book. I am interested in your opinion on which of the magical locations you would like to visit the most. And which product would you buy first?

1. HOUSES

4 Privet Drive

4 Privet Drive is the address of the home of Petunia Dursley, Harry Potter's own aunt on his mother's side, who lives in Little Whinging with her husband and son.

It was here that Rubeus Hagrid brought the one-year-old Harry from his destroyed parental home in Godric's Hollow at the request of Albus Dumbledore. Harry lived here for ten years until he found out that he was a wizard, and he returned here every year for the summer holidays; it was this house that he called his home until he came of age. And, although this house did not become native to him, it still reliably protected Harry Potter from Voldemort and his henchmen.

It is noteworthy that until the age of eleven, Harry lived in a closet under the stairs. And this is when there were two spare bedrooms in the house: one was kept by the Dursleys for guests, and the other was used by Dudley as his personal pantry. Only after the letters from Hogwarts arrived was the orphan given the smallest bedroom, which angered his cousin to the core. And this anger arose not because Harry was given a small room but because it was given at all.

But even after Harry had a normal room, he did not feel safe in it. Not only does he always look back at his uncle and aunt (suddenly, they will hear the scratching of a pen on parchment, but suddenly they will see a strip of light from under the door); sometimes the Dursleys behave like real jailers. Enraged that the deal with Mason broke down because of HarryUncle Vernon put a grate on the window of his twelve-year-old nephew and made a small door for food in the door. Now Harry was only allowed out of the room to go to the toilet. Isn't it a prison? So the escape from the house, arranged for Potter by the Weasley brothers, was a real escape.

Three years later, the Dursleys tried to lock Harry in his room again. However, having formally secured his consent, again, the nephew left the house without asking. And again, not without outside help.

And yet, leaving the house on Privet Drive forever, Harry remembers the pleasant moments associated with this place. There weren't that many of them, but they were there (albeit mostly in the absence of the Dursleys) ...

Author's comment

The name of the street where the Dursleys live is a reference to the most suburban plant, the privet bush, which neatly encloses many English gardens. I loved the association with both the suburb and the fence because the Dursleys are such a smug middle class, and they are so decisively walled off from the wizarding world. The name of this area is "Little Whinging," which again sounds rather limited and contemptuous, "whinging" is the colloquial form of "complain or whine" in British English.

Despite the fact that I described the Dursleys ' house as large and square, befitting Uncle Vernon's status as a company director, whenever I made descriptions, I unconsciously imagined my second house, where I lived as a child. My house was on the contrary very small with three bedrooms. I first realized this when I entered the home in 4 Privet Drive, which was built at Leavesden Film Studios and found myself in an exact copy of my old house, starting from the placement of the closet under the stairs and ending with the exact location of each room. I never described my old home to a set designer, director, or producer, it was another disturbing experience that filming Potter brought me.

For no particular reason, I never liked the number 4, which always turned out to be difficult and inexorable for me, which is why I slapped it directly on the front door of the Dursleys' house.

The Burrow

The Burrow is the home of the Weasley family of pureblood wizards.

Location

The Burrow is located near the village of Ottery St Catchpole, located in the south-west of England, in the county of Devonshire. The house is protected by Muggle-repellent spells, so the Muggle postmen do not know about its existence.

Not far from the Weasley house are other families of wizards: the Lovegood, the Fawcett and the Diggory. During its existence, the Burrow has been home to Arthur, Molly Weasley and their children. Harry Potter, Hermione Granger and some members of the Order of the Phoenix also visited the house.

In the place where the Burrow now stands, there used to be a small Tudor house with a brick pigsty. Therefore, when the young Weasley couple bought this house, we can say that they settled in a pigsty. Apparently, initially, the house was smaller than the current one, but with the appearance of each next child in the family, new rooms were added to it, expanding the house, acquiring new premises. By 1990, the house already had several floors, with five chimneys on a red tiled roof and was probably strengthened with the help of magic.

The Weasley Family Home

The Weasleys are believed to have lived at the Burrow for a long time, at least since 1970. The Burrow was home to nine members of the Weasley family, although their numbers began to thin out as the children grew up and left home. Despite their poverty, none of the Weasleys seem to be ashamed of their home. It was a wonderful place, where there was a cozy and relaxed atmosphere; a friendly house in which family friends were frequent guests.

In the summer of 1992, Harry Potter visited the Burrow for the first time, when Ron, Fred and George Weasley "kidnapped" him from the Dursleys ' house. He stayed with them throughout the summer and began to treat the Burrow as his second home after Hogwarts, while Arthur and Molly Weasley began to perceive him as another son and family member during this time.

Interior

The interior of the Burrow is comfortable, although the furniture is very diverse: you will not find two things made in the same style here.

Behind the scenes

In the German translation, the Burrow is translated as "Fuchsbau" — "Fox Hole," which causes an association with the fiery red hair of the Weasley family.

Hagrid's Hut

Hagrid's Hut is a small house located in the east of the Hogwarts territory, between the castle and Forbidden Forest, near the Main Gate. It is home to the school forester Rubeus Hagrid. Probably, Hagrid's predecessor, the forest ranger Ogg, used to live in it. The hut consists of two small rooms: a common room and a storage room. The hut is a little cramped, but there is enough space for a half-giant. Moreover, sometimes Hagrid settles especially dear little animals next to him. Like, for example, the Buckbeak hippogriff, not to mention Rubeus ' constant companion, the over-sized dog "Fang." In the larger room, there is a table, chairs and Hagrid's bed, there is also a fireplace, where Rubeus cooks simple food for himself and manages to bake cupcakes (although they're not quite edible). In the same fireplace, he nursed a dragon egg.

There is a small vegetable garden next to the dwelling, where the forester grows a variety of vegetables, as well as pumpkins for Halloween. The lodge is clearly visible from the Gryffindor and astronomical towers. Harry Potter, Ron Weasley and Hermione Granger were often there.

Differences

Although the hut is made of stone in the film, it is wooden in the book. At least this can be understood when Hermione warns Hagrid about the dangers of keeping the dragon in the house.

12 Grimmauld Place

12 Grimmauld Place is owned by the Black family. At the time this house appeared in the narrative, the last representative of this family, Sirius Black, lived here. Sirius ' father had once cast all the protective spells he knew on this ancient house. The house is absent from all maps, both Muggle and magical; the house cannot be seen, and what happens in it cannot be heard. It is also impossible to smell or touch it, to detect it with the help of devices and even spells. And after Albus Dumbledore put a Trust spell ("Fidelius") on the house, there is probably no safer place to find in the whole of England.

Facade

A house with dirty walls and blackened windows. The entrance to the building is decorated with a porch with worn stone steps. The battered door is painted black, the paint has cracked over time and crumbled in places. The door has neither a keyhole nor a letter box, but there is a silver door knocker in the shape of a writhing snake. On the inside, the door is equipped with metal locks and a chain. The door hinges have not been lubricated for a long time, so they creak.

Things of the house Black

In the old house, not only family heirlooms were kept, like porcelain, the family rings, or an old watch, but in unexpected places in the house, you could find dark artifacts. At first glance, it was impossible to assume that they were dangerous. For example, the purple robe hanging in the closet among other robes almost strangled Ron Weasley during cleaning. Or silver tweezers, biting the first one who touched them. And the luxurious medallion with the emerald snake depicted on it turned out to be not just a decoration but the legacy of Salazar Slytherin and the horcrux of Voldemort. The last representative of the Black family simply threw away almost all of his luxurious property.

Malfoy Manor

Malfoy Manor is an old mansion and parkland in Wiltshire owned by the old Malfoy family and passed down from generation to generation.

The territory of the estate

A wide hedge-lined driveway leads to the estate. At the entrance, there is a high forged gate made

I look like Harry Potter if instead of going to wizard school, he just kept living under the stairs.

JOKES HP

On the central High Street of Hogsmeade is a Honeydukes confectionery, several funny souvenir shops, a Scrivenshaft writing supplies store, an owl post office and several beer bars, the most popular of which is the Three Broomsticks. The owner of the Three Broomsticks, Madame Rosmerte, and the owner of the Hog's Head Inn, Aberforth Dumbledore, also live in Hogsmeade.

Another attraction of Hogsmeade is Shrieking Shack, located on the outskirts of the village, but the villagers prefer not to approach it.

Any Hogwarts student, starting from the third year, gets the right to attend Hogsmeade on weekends, if the parents or guardian provide the school administration with written permission. For bad behavior, a student may be deprived of this right by the dean of the faculty or other representative of the school leadership. For example, in the third year, on the initiative of Professor McGonagall, Neville Longbottom lost this right by the end of the year due to negligence, after losing a piece of paper with passwords from the portrait to the living room.In the fifth year, Harry Potter was deprived of this opportunity on the initiative of Inspector General Umbridge for giving an interview about the revival of Voldemort for the Quibble magazine in Hogsmeade.

It is known that in this village there was a cottage in which Elphinstone Urquart and Minerva McGonagall lived in the 1980s. After Urquart's death, McGonagall sold the house and moved to Hogwarts.

Hogsmeade Station

Hogsmeade is the name not only of the village but also of the nearest railway station to Hogwarts. To get to Hogsmeade station, you need to take the Hogwarts Express train, which departs from King's Cross Station in London, from platform 9¾. Platform 9¾ can also be accessed by passing through the brick wall separating Platforms 9 and 10. (Platforms 9 and 10 at King's Cross Station in London do exist).

Behind the scenes

At the Wizarding World of Harry Potter, a theme park in Orlando, there is Hogsmeade with its main establishments.

Little Hangleton

Little Hangleton is a small village perched between two hills, on one of which stands the Riddle house. The Riddle themselves have not lived there for a very long time. In the summer of 1943, they were all found dead. The police never found the killer, to be honest, they didn't even find the cause of death: Mr. Riddle, his wife and their son were absolutely healthy at the time of death. The house has since changed several owners, but none of them lived there for a long time. The last owner of the Riddle house did not appear there at all.

The remains of the Riddle family are buried in the local cemetery, and on their grave, according to the film, there is a stone statue of death with a scythe. It was here, at the grave of his father, that Voldemort was reborn. Here, in front of his loyal Death Eaters, he staged a duel with the young Harry Potter.

There is another attraction in Little Hangleton, but few residents know about it, and those who know, do not consider it a landmark: just an old dilapidated shack. But it was here that the family of the Gaun lived, the last direct descendants of one of the founders of Hogwarts, Salazar Slytherin. The fate of these people is sad. In 1926, Merope Gaunt ran away with the son of the owners of the Riddle house, Tom, who then abandoned her pregnant. After giving birth to a child, she died in a Muggle orphanage. Marvolo Gaunt survived his daughter by only a few years, and Morphine Gaunt ended his days in Azkaban for a murder he did not commit.

3. PRISONS

Azkaban

Azkaban is a prison for wizards who have violated the laws of the magical world, guarded by Dementors.

Wizards who violate the laws of the magical community of Great Britain are imprisoned in it (it is not quite clear whether there are criminals from other countries there, but this option seems quite likely). The most famous guards of the prison are Dementors, subordinate to the Ministry of Magic. (Most likely, there are other guards; it is who deals with the distribution of prisoners to cells and controls that prisoners are released on time after serving their prison term — the Dementors, according to Hagrid, do not want to voluntarily release anyone). As a rule, wizards who have committed serious crimes get into Azkaban. Many of the prisoners are supporters of Lord Voldemort.

The prison building is a tall, triangular tower in cross-section. The walls of the prison are thick, fortified, but it is quite possible to destroy them, although, it probably needs strong magic for this.

History

Azkaban has been known to wizards since the 15th century, but it was not immediately used as a prison. Until that time, no one had heard anything about Azkaban, the island had never been mapped to the geographical maps of both sorcerers and Muggles. It is believed that this island in the North Sea, like the fortress erected on it, was created with the help of magic.

Initially, the fortress served as the home of a sorcerer named Ekrizdis, about whom little is known. We do not know what country this wizard was from. One thing is clear: he was a powerful magician who practiced the worst types of dark magic. Ekrizdis lived completely alone on an island in the middle of the ocean, and in order to somehow entertain himself, he lured Muggle sailors, and then tortured and killed them. It was only after his death, when the disguising spell was dispelled, that the Ministry of Magic discovered the island and the structure erected on it. The people investigating the case declined to comment on what they found inside the fortress. All this was further overshadowed by the fact that the island was filled with Dementors.

Many reputable wizards were sure that the island was the abode of evil, and the best solution would be to destroy it. Others were afraid of what could happen if such a large number of Dementors were deprived of their homes. They were already so strong that it was not possible to destroy them; many were afraid that the Dementors would take revenge if they were deprived of the home they were used to. It seemed that the walls of the building, as if soaked with suffering and pain, were holding the Dementors. In addition, experts studying buildings erected with the help of dark magic argued that the destruction of Azkaban could end badly. Therefore, the fortress remained intact, and to this day, serves as a habitat for Dementors.

Reputation

In the wizarding world, Azkaban prison is justifiably considered a terrible place. The prison is guarded by a lot of Dementors, who, as you know, magically pull out all the bright emotions from a person and make them relive all the worst memories. Sirius Black said that many prisoners simply stopped eating and died of hunger. Most likely, Azkaban is not the only prison for wizards. But other prisons are hardly mentioned. Is that the prison where Nurmengard became a personal prison for Gellert Grindelwald.

Nurmengard

Nurmengard is a prison in the Alps created by Gellert Grindelwald. It was built for the purpose of imprisoning the ideological enemies of Grindelwald. On the gates of Nurmengard, the inscription is engraved: "For the common good" and a drawing symbolizing the Deathly Hallows. After being defeated in a duel with Dumbledore, Grindelwald was imprisoned in a prison created for his own enemies.

4. STREETS, SHOPS AND CAFES

Diagon Alley

Diagon Alley is a winding street in the magical world, paved with cobblestones, stretching from northwest to northeast. The center of magic goods. It'a the only place in London where you can buy a magical animal, a flying broom, a wand and many other magical things and magical goods. The English branch of Gringotts Wizarding Bank, is also located in Diagon Alley. You can go to the alley through the Leaky Cauldron cafe, which is Muggles located on Charing Cross Road. You can also get into it with the help of volatile gunpowder through the fireplace network, moving to one of the fireplaces, usually in the Leaky Cauldron. However, on the first attempt to get there in this way, Harry missed and landed in Knockturn Alley, which is adjacent to Diagon Alley. Knockturn Alley stores, unlike Diagon stores, specialize in dark magic and dark artifacts.

History

According to a popular historical theory, the oldest building in Diagon Alley is the Magic Gringotts Bank, around which the store buildings were later built. However, there is also the possibility that Ollivander's shop is the oldest building. At least, according to the inscription on the sign, the foundation of this company dates back to the end of the fourth century BC.

Main shops, shops and cafes

1. **Mr. Mulpepper's Apothecary** is a pharmacy where you can buy various potions and ingredients for them.

2. **Slug & Jigger's** is a store founded in 1207. Here, you can buy potions and ingredients for them. It is located next door to its competitor - Mr. Mulpepper's Apothecary.

3. **Weasleys' Wizard Wheeze**s - a store of humor goods from Fred and George Weasley.

4. **Quality Quidditch Supplies** — a store for buying flying brooms and all kinds of Quidditch accessories.

5. **Wiseacre's Wizarding Equipment** is a store that sells a variety of magical tools, such as telescopes and hourglasses. It first appeared in the film "Harry Potter and the Chamber of Secrets." There is also a local branch in Hogsmeade.

6. **The Magical Menagerie** is a store that sells not only owls but also many other animals.

7. **Gringotts Wizard Bank** is a magic bank.

8. **The Leaky Cauldron** is a popular pub located on the London side of Charing Cross Road. You can go through the backyard of the pub into Diagon Alley by touching the brick above the urn three times with the magic wand ("Three up ... two to the side ...") and opening the arch.

9. **Obscurus Books** is a publishing house that publishes various magical books, including such a popular one as "Fantastic Beasts and Where to Find Them." The main office is located at 18a, on the south side of Diagon Alley.

10. **Sugarplum's Sweetshop** is a store that sells pastries, such as licorice wands and pumpkin pies.

11. **Gambol & Japes Wizarding Joke Shop** is a magic joke store that also sells magic crackers. It's the favorite store of Fred and George Weasley and their buddy Lee Jordan.

12. **Ollivander's Wand Shop**. The Ollivanders are the best wandmakers in England. The surname of these masters has been known for more than 2000 years.

13. **Scribbulus Writing Implements** is a shop that sells writing materials. In this shop, Hagrid helped Harry buy everything he needed for writing when he visited Diagon Alley for the first time. In the second year, Hermione Granger dragged Ron away from the Quidditch shop and dragged him to this shop for shopping.

14. **Potage's Cauldron Shop** — here, you can buy a cauldron of any size made of copper, bronze, tin, silver and gold. Two types of boilers are offered — self-stirring and collapsible. It's the nearest store to the exit of the Leaky Cauldron. A certain number of products are displayed right in front of the store.

15. **Madam Malkin's Robes for all Occasions**-clothing store. Usually, Hogwarts students buy school robes here, which Madam Malkin can immediately adjust to size.

16. **Flourish & Blotts** is a popular bookstore. It also sells textbooks that are used to study at Hogwarts.

Knockturn Alley

Knockturn Alley is adjacent to Diagon Alley and occupies a smaller area. This is a crooked, darkened street with shops selling dark artifacts and ingredients for dark magic. The most famous of them is the Borgin and Burkes shop. Wizards who use the services of such institutions usually prefer not to advertise this.

Famous Knockturn Alley Establishments:

1. **The White Wyvern** is a pub.

2. **Betting shop** is an organization that accepts bets on various sports events. Presumably, there could be bets on a game of Quidditch.

3. **Borgin and Burkes** is the most famous institution in London, engaged in buying and selling strong and noticeable magical things, mainly related to dark magic. It is also possible that dark ingredients also fall on the store counter. However, in Borgin and Burkes, sometimes quite harmless things come across.

4. **Chimney Sweep Elf** is an organization where it was possible to rent a House-elf to clean the chimney.

5. **Ye Olde Curiosity Shop** - A shop that sold dark arts-related items.

6. **Noggin and Bonce** is a store specializing in the sale of dried heads (you can notice this when passing by the main showcase).

7. **Trackleshanks Locksmith** is a shop where you can buy and install locks or replace keys.

8. **Markus Scarrs Indelible Tattoos** – a wymagic tattoo parlor.

BONUS. HOMEMADE BUTTERBEER RECIPE

Those who love the Butterbeer from Wizarding World of Harry Potter would also love the taste of this beverage. They are lucky to have this recipe.

What is Butterbeer?

Those who are not fans of Harry Potter must be wondering what Butterbeer is and what is so special about it? So, it is a cold, frothy, and sweet drink, which tastes like butter and cream soda that was made in the world of Harry Potter. The Butterbeer is made from the description given in the book series.

In the books, Harry and his friends get the privilege of going to a place near their wizarding school called Hogsmeade. In Hogsmeade, their favorite place to grab a treat is called The Three Broomsticks, where they enjoy a cold, delicious Butterbeer every time.

Is Butterbeer Alcoholic?

The Butterbeer described in the book may give a buzz to the one who drinks it. But the Butterbeer which is made at Universal theme park or the one described here does not contain any alcohol.

Turn Frozen Butterbeer Into An Alcoholic Beverage

Yet, if you want to make it alcoholic, just add ½ cup of vodka or rum to make it alcoholic. After adding, mix it thoroughly.

You can also add rum extract to give it a rum flavor without making it alcoholic. You just need to add one teaspoon of rum extract and blend it.

How to Make Butterbeer

STEP 1

Place the following in a blender:

➢ 8 ice cubes
➢ Half a 1.75-quart container of vanilla ice cream
➢ 3 cups of cream soda (24 oz.)
➢ 6 oz. butterscotch topping (found in the ice cream toppings section)
➢ Puree until smooth.

STEP 2

Pour your drink into the glass, top it with whipped cream if you like and drizzle some syrup of butterscotch. Must serve immediately!

With a cup of BUTTERBEER, it will be more fun to read the book! Bon appetit ;)

37 INTERESTING FACTS

Everyone knows the story of Harry Potter, but few people know what happened behind the scenes of the movies or what inspired JK Rowling to write one of the most widely read book series in the world.

These little-known facts about Harry Potter will throw you off the broom and give you a glimpse into the makings of a series that changed the future of children's literature and made the Muggle world a little more magical. Although the beloved series has officially come to an end, for the Harry Potter generation, this story will live forever. Enjoy HP Facts.

1. We can see the picture of Gandalf the Grey (from The Lord of the Rings) in the collection of amazing wizards in Professor Dumbledore's study in the Harry Potter and the Chamber of Secrets.

2. In 2007, Rowling made it to the Time magazine's Person of the Year, yet stayed runner up.

3. A 37-year-old actress who played Moaning Myrtle is the oldest of all actresses/actors portraying a Hogwarts student.

4. Rowling's mother died of sclerosis, which left a significant influence on her writing; hence death remains the prominent theme throughout the Harry Potter series.

5. In Harry Potter and the Sorcerer's Stone, the blood of the dragon is a very effective oven cleaner.

6. Rowling's books were the first children's books to be on the New York Bestseller list after Charlotte's Web by E.B. White in 1952.

7. When Harry Potter and the Prisoner of Azkaban was released in Great Britain, the publisher asked stores not to sell the book until schools were closed for the day to prevent truancy.

8. The first Harry Potter manuscript was rejected by many publishers who said it was too long and literary, yet it was accepted by the Bloomsbury Publisher in 1996. The book's publisher suggested that Rowling use the name "J. K." instead of her real name, "Joanne Rowling," in order to appeal to men readers. She borrowed "K" from her grandmother as her name was Kathleen, although her legal name doesn't contain "Kathleen," not even "K."

9. Rowling's series made children read. It also gave way to boost the sale of other children's literature, for instance, The Chronicles of Narnia series of C.S. Lewis and The Black Cauldron series of Lloyd Alexander.

10. Rowling once said that she might have borrowed the name of Harry's school, "Hogwarts" via a Hogwarts plant she witnessed in New York City's Kew Gardens.

11. Black tattoos of Sirius are borrowed from the prison gangs of Russia. The person identified through markings is someone to be feared but respected.

12. Emma Watson, Daniel Radcliffe, and Rupert Grint were asked by the director of The Prisoner of Azkaban to write essays from the perspectives of the characters. Radcliffe wrote one page, Watson wrote a 10-page essay, and Grint didn't write anything.

13. King's Cross station is visited by lots of fans. They take pictures of platforms 9 and 10 that are erected by the station management, a sign that says "Platform 9 ¾," which is invisible to Muggles in the Potter books, but it acts as a fine gateway for witches and wizards.

14. The Latin motto of The Hogwarts school is Draco dormiens nunquam titillandus, which means "Never Tickle a Sleeping Dragon."

15. In the novels, Hogwarts is situated somewhere in Scotland, and it has various charms to look like an old ruin in the eyes of muggles.

16. The first person to become a billionaire (U.S. dollars) by writing books is none other than J. K. Rowling.

17. Members of the Jesus Non- Denominational Church of Greenville, Michigan, demonstrated for what they considered evil in Harry Potter books in 2003. They gathered a bonfire and burnt Rowling's books. Burning books used to be a radical statement during the Middle Ages when books were rare.

18. To Rowling, the phoenix is her favorite beast in the series, which is a mythical sacred bird who explodes into fires when it gets 500 or 1,000 years old just to originate from the flames as a new and young phoenix.

19. To make the school setting more real, the young actors had to do their actual homework in the Harry Potter movies.

20. Both Rosie O'Donnell and Robin Williams offered to be in the Harry Potter film without pay. However, they were declined because she wanted a predominantly British/Irish cast.

21. During the filming of the Harry Potter movies, Daniel Radcliffe broke almost 80 wands because he used them as drumsticks.

22. The pet snowy owl of the Harry Potter Hedwig is actually named after two very famous saints from the 11th & 12th centuries. One of the Saints, Hedwig of Andechs (1174-1243) is a former duchess known for her munificence and sympathetic nature. The other one is Saint Hedwig, who was the Queen of Poland (1373 to 1399). Harry's loss of innocence and coming of age is manifested by the death of Hedwig in Harry Potter and the Deathly Hallows.

23. Real food was served at the dining hall in the Sorcerer's Stone.

24. In 2003, Harry Potter and the Order of the Phoenix sold as many as 5 million copies in the first 24 hours of the beginning of their sale. In 2005, on the first day of its release, Half-Blood Prince sold a record-breaking 11 million copies, while Harry Potter and the Deathly Hallows sold more than 15 million copies globally.

25. The Harry Potter books are one of the most translated books in history after having been translated into 70 languages.

26. The moving candles in the Great Hall were made by using candle-shaped holders consisting of oil and burning wicks. These were adjourned from wires that moved up and down in an interesting manner in order to create the impression that these were floating. Subsequently, once a wire cracked because of the heat of the fire/flame, which caused the candle to fall to the floor straight away. It was fortunate that no one was injured, but later, it was decided that the candles would be recreated using CGI for the upcoming films as the use of real candles was possibly a severe safety hazard.

27. The height of Hagrid is 8 feet 6 inches.

28. The problem creator ghost Peeves, which was played by Rik Mayall, is not shown at the end of the movie nor in the deleted scenes on all the home editions of Potter movie. According to Mayall, he didn't know that he was cut from the final cut until he watched the movie. Ultimately, the Harry Potter films never used Peeves anymore.

29. Rowling made it clear that if Voldemort ever saw a boggart, it would consequently embody his corpse because his greatest fear was always death.

30. An old English word for "bumblebee" is Dumbledore. According to Rowling, the name was chosen because she depicted Dumbledore whining to himself.

31. Rowling once claimed that she almost broke her promise to herself in keeping the Golden Trio alive and killed Ron in the midst of the series at a time when she "wasn't in a very happy place" of her life. She later confessed that she wouldn't have really done it, but at the time, she thought it "out of sheer spite."

32. Prisoner of Azkaban aimed to stop sneaking food on set by sewing shut the pockets of Tom Felton's Hogwarts; it has been shown while filming him.

33. Harry and Ron saved Hermione from the troll in the bathroom on the 10th death anniversary of Harry's parents' and the first time Voldemort was defeated, 31st October 1991. This is the day the trio became friends for real.

34. Trelawney, in Prisoner of Azkaban, refused to sit at a place with the other 12 characters for she would be the 13th. This would make him the first one to get up after that shall die. In Order of the Phoenix, among the 13 members of the order sitting, the Sirius was the first who stood.

35. When Rowling had finished writing half of Goblet of Fire, she realised that she had created a big hole in its plot. She had to go back and fix that giant hole in the plot, which is why the book is that much longer.

36. Rowling spent the first five years on Harry Potter fixing the rules about the domains of her characters and what they could and could not do.

37. Rowling published her first Harry Potter in 1998, which was the year when the final Battle of Hogwarts happened. Rowling noted the following, "I open at the close."

12 SUBTLE DETAILS IN HARRY POTTER MOVIES

Movies often include minute details that only true lovers of literature and fantasy can spot. Here, we have highlighted 12 brilliant details that were subtly placed in the Harry Potter Movies. Let's put on our detective caps and dive right in.

1. Remember in Part 2 of Deathly Hollow after Voldemort reveals that Harry's dead? Well, the moment we discover that Harry is actually alive, George Weasley briefly relays this information to Fred who's standing next to him out of excitement. It happens for a brief moment.

2. Another brilliant detail that we can't seem to get over in the Harry Potter Films is the changes made to Voldemort's Robes. Every time a Horcrux was destroyed, the color of his robes faded. This simple detail was a symbolic representation of how Voldemort's life was gradually coming to an end.

3. Harry Potter and the Sorcerer's Stone (2001) subtly made reference to Anne Boleyn, the wife of Henry VIII, with her picture hanging in the staircase. She was executed on account of being a witch.

4. The Harry Potter movie intros went from less intense to much darker as the stories got darker.

5. At the End Credits Of 'Goblet of Fire', the Harry Potter crew added a Magical Disclaimer that read. 'No Dragons Were Harmed in the Making of This Movie'. This action is probably the crew's effort to let viewers know that even magical creatures, like real-life animals used in movies, are also safe. Bet you didn't notice that.

6. Remember in 'The Sorcerer's Stone' Scene, where Neville gets a Remembrall, that reminds him that he forgot something, but he didn't seem to remember what he forgets? Well, although we weren't told what he forgot, we can deduce from that scene that he probably forgot to wear his robe. This is the reason why he is the only student without his robe at the dinner table.

7. In 'The Sorcerer's Stone, when Hermonie shows Harry his dad's name, John Potter, on the Quidditch, Mcgonagall's Name is the Quidditch Trophy Next To James Potter's. Her name is accompanied by the year she was awarded.

8. Daniel Radcliffe brought the idea of Harry wearing a Button-down sweater at Day Meetings in Harry Potter and the Order of the Phoenix (2007). The idea was for Harry Potter to imitate the looks of his favorite teacher.

9. Although we were officially introduced to the character of Newt Scamander in Fantastic beasts and where to find them, he had a cameo appearance in the 'Prisoner Of Azkaban'. We see his name on the Marauder's Map.

10. To buttress the point that Hermione, Ron, and Harry have been traveling for long in search of the Horcruxes in the first part of the Deathly Hallows, Hermione Granger's hair grows all through the movie.

11. Harry Potter's rare gift as a Seeker is predicted by his ability to keep his eyes fixed on the snitch. While Oliver Wood taught Harry how to play the Quidditch, he Releases the Snitch. Although he wasn't able to keep up with the Snitch, Harry was able to keep his gaze fixated on it.

12. In 'The Sorcerer's Stone, ' a scene from the Harry Potter books, was directly replicated. It is the scene where Aunt Petunia uses a dye to change Dudley's old clothes to gray for Harry's school uniform.

CHARACTERS

This section of the book describes the main characters of the series of novels (which significantly influenced the plot of the works).

Characters creation and real world influence

Several characters and magical creatures in the series of novels created by J.K. Rowling are associated with mythical characters who were mentioned before her. These characters include centaurs, basilisk, phoenix, acromantula, unicorns, etc.

Some of the main characters of the Harry Potter books appeared due to events that took place in the writer's life. For example, according to some sources, Rowling partly borrowed the appearance of Harry Potter from her old friend Ian Potter, with whom she played wizards at the age of 2-7 when she lived in Winterbourne, although the writer herself confirms this fact, then denies it. The prototype of Aunt Marge Dursley was Joan's maternal grandmother Frida Volant: according to the writer, her marriage to grandfather Ernie was "unsuccessful," and she called the atmosphere that reigned in their house "chaos."

In one of the episodes of the book "Harry Potter and the Goblet of Fire," freshman Natalie MacDonald appears. She got her name in honor of a real girl who wrote a letter to J. K. Rowling, because she was ill with cancer and was afraid to wait for the release of the book "Harry Potter and the Goblet of Fire." She really wanted to know what would happen to Harry Potter in the new book and asked the writer to tell her about it. Unfortunately, Joan was not looking through the mail at that time, because she was finishing work on a book, so the answer was late, and the girl died without knowing what would happen to Harry. Joan gave the heroine of the book the name of this girl and visited her parents, giving them an autographed book.

Please do not forget to leave reviews about the book! I wonder which of the characters you like the most? And who made the greatest contribution to the victory over Voldemort?

1. GRYFFINDOR STUDENTS

Harry James Potter

"And now, Harry, let us step out into the night and pursue that flighty temptress, adventure."

— Albus Dumbledore

HP Quotes

Harry James Potter is the main character, classmate and best friend of Ronald Weasley and Hermione Granger, a member of the Golden Trio. He's the most famous student of Hogwarts in the last hundred years and the first wizard who managed to resist the deadly curse of Avada Kedavra, thanks to which he became famous and received the nickname The Boy Who Lived. He fought heroically against Lord Voldemort and his followers, the Death Eaters.

Appearance

Harry Potter outwardly is a spitting image of his father (for Sirius, like a resurrected friend), only his green eyes are similar to those of his mother (in the film, the actor who plays Harry Potter, Daniel Radcliffe, has blue eyes). Harry is small and thin, he looks a little younger than his age, with black, always tousled hair, a thin face and protruding knees. He wears round glasses. Harry has the famous lightning-shaped scar on his forehead.

Character

At the beginning of the story, Harry is a lonely, withdrawn child, who is constantly humiliated in his family and at school. The difficult life at the Dursleys forms in him such a trait as distrust. When Hagrid appears in his life, the boy doubts what is happening to the last.

In the first year of study at Hogwarts, where Harry finally feels like a full-fledged person, the main traits of his character, both positive and negative, are determined.

Harry is kind, takes any human relationship seriously, will never betray a loved one, treats adults with respect, who, of course, have earned this respect. He never attacks first; on the contrary, he often has to fend off attacks himself. Harry is a leader by nature, and if he has to lead something (be the captain of the Quidditch team or the head of Dumbledore's Army), he is pretty good at it. Harry never boasts of his fame; on the contrary, his own fame irritates him. He is not sociable, and even though he inevitably has to contact a large number of people, he has close relationships with only a few. Harry is quite secretive and never shares his feelings and experiences with even close friends.

Harry Potter is a "first impression person." If he didn't like someone (or vice versa, liked them) at first sight, he is very reluctant to reconsider his attitude towards that person. However, he always easily and even happily forgives the offender, if only he would say: "I'm sorry, Harry, I was deeply wrong." So it happened with Ron and a year later with Seamus, then with Dudley... Harry cannot abstract from his own emotions and rely only on facts like Remus Lupin, he does not know how to tenaciously notice details like Hermione Granger, he does not know how to treat everything with humor like the Weasley twins. But on the other hand, he is able to deeply and strongly love people and anticipate things that cannot be explained in words. "Always follow your intuition," Lupin once tells him, " it almost never deceives you."

Hermione Jean Granger

Hermione Granger is a friend and classmate of Harry Potter and Ron Weasley. The only daughter of Mr. Granger and his wife.

At the age of eleven, the girl learns that she is actually a sorceress and is enrolled in Hogwarts. She plays an important role in all the events that occur in Harry's life. Hermione, apparently, is the oldest among her classmates — she was born on September 19, 1979 and could not enter Hogwarts a year earlier since a student must be fully eleven years old at the time of admission. Most of her classmates were born in 1980.

Hermione loves studying very much and devotes a lot of time to it. Sometimes, she is too arrogant and overly proud of her academic success. She is ambitious, and in the classroom, she always tries to answer first and stand out with her knowledge, for which many consider her a "know-it-all." In the eyes of those around her, with her fanatical desire for order and discipline, she looks too "correct" and boring. However, the first impression about her turns out to be wrong. Indeed, compliance with formal rules and academic success means a lot to her, but we can say with all confidence that there are much more significant values and ideals for her.

Studying at Hogwarts

Her favorite subject is Charms (later-Arithmetic). And only some things (Flying and Divination) caused certain difficulties. Once, she admitted that Sorting Hat first offered her to study at the Ravenclaw faculty (where the smartest students study), but then changed her mind and sent her to Gryffindor.

After entering Hogwarts, Hermione shared a room with Lavender Brown, Parvati Patil and two other Gryffindor girls.

Due to her responsibility, good academic performance and exemplary behavior, in her fifth year, Hermione was appointed head of the faculty.

Magic Power and Skills

Hermione's observation is amazing. For example, she is the only one who notices what Fluffy is standing on, while Harry and Ron are not taking their eyes off the three scary monster heads. One glance at the luggage of the teacher sleeping in the compartment is enough for her to see Professor Lupine's mark. While everyone's attention is focused on the Goblet of Fire, which suddenly decides to throw out the name of the fourth Champion, Hermione peers at Harry. The expression on her friend's face leaves no doubt: the choice of the Goblet for Harry is a complete surprise. For a very long time, until the end of the first round of the Triwizard Tournament, Hermione remained almost the only Hogwarts student who did not accuse Potter of cheating.

Hermione is a brave and courageous girl who is ready to help her friends anytime, anywhere. Nevertheless, we can say that one of her weaknesses is the inability to act in a non-standard situation when you need to make a quick decision. Over the years, this feature of her also changes. We can say that Hermione's tenacious observation is gradually being replaced by the ability to quickly navigate the situation. If she is given at least a minute to think calmly, she will find the best solution.

Her slender figure and small stature (in The Deathly Hallows, it is mentioned that Hermione is shorter than Harry, who is shorter than Ron) give her an advantage in ranged combat — in books and movies, there is not a single case that an enemy could hit her with any spell unless he was close enough. Her long hair also has a special property: they never interfere with her, they don't cling to anything, and no one manages to grab her for them.

Ron Weasley

Ronald Bilius "Ron" Weasley is one of the main characters, friend and classmate of Harry Potter and Hermione Granger, the youngest son of the Weasley family.

Character

Ron is the youngest son in the Weasley family. He has five older brothers (Charlie, Bill, Percy, twins Fred and George) and a younger sister Ginny. Ron's mother's habit of setting older children as an example to younger ones has developed a kind of "second-rate" complex in him, which he keenly experiences, trying to surpass his older brothers. The fact that Hermione is studying better than him in all subjects, and Harry is becoming more famous every year makes Ron look for different ways to achieve this goal.

Ron's biggest fear is spiders. And there is a reason for this: long ago, as a child, one of the Weasley twins turned Ron's teddy bear into a giant spider. Since then, even harmless house spiders have caused him to panic. However, despite his fears, Ron is able to sacrifice himself for the well-being of loved ones. He becomes brave and selfless when friends need help.

Because of his frivolous attitude to school, Ron seems lazy and childish. Hermione described him as an immature person, unable to guess about the feelings of others. Knowing how to defuse the situation at the right time, Harry Potter's best friend has a special perception of morality, often offending comrades.

Appearance

In the books, Ron is described as a thin and lanky boy with red hair and blue eyes, and his face is covered with freckles. Of all the brothers, he is the most similar in build to Percy.

Magic Power and Skills

Interestingly, Ron's powers are most clearly manifested in those moments when he feels responsible for someone else. He perfectly applied the Wingardium Leviosa charm, saving Hermione from the troll and Harry helplessly hanging on the troll. But a couple of hours ago, he did not work out at all! He defended Tonks during Operation The Seven Potters, sitting on a broom behind her back. And Nymphadora spoke of him with genuine admiration: it's so cool to use spells on a moving target!

Behind the scenes

1. Ron was one of the few characters that appeared in JK Rowling's head long before the book series began, and she always knew that he would be named Ron Weasley.

2. In one of the chapters, Professor Slughorn accidentally calls Ron the future name of the actor who plays him - Rupert.

3. The choice of Ron's patronus - a terrier dog-is not accidental. Joan had a terrier, and she found it very touching.

4. According to Rowling, she and Ron would have the same Boggart-spiders since she also can't stand them.

Ginny Weasley

Ginevra Molly "Ginny" Weasley; August 11, 1981 - one of the main characters in the Harry Potter book series. The seventh child of the Weasleys and the first girl in generations.

A short, slender, beautiful girl with bright light brown eyes and red straight hair, a talented, strong sorceress and athlete.

A long-awaited daughter in the family, Ginny has always enjoyed a little more attention and care from her mother. However, she did not grow up to be a spoiled girl or one who followed strictly established norms and rules. Many years later, Hermione let slip that Ginny had been sneaking Fred and George's brooms out of the barn to fly since she was six. For as long as she can remember, Ginny has always wanted to go to Hogwarts and was looking forward to this day. Every year, she accompanied her brothers to school.

Magic Power and Skills

Ginny Weasley has a special talent for defending against the Dark Arts. From the very first classes in D.A. under the leadership of Harry, she was noted as one of the best. Ginny's talent was also noted by Professor Slughorn and Aberforth Dumbledore. He is proficient in the Bat-Bogey Hex spell. Ginny has a fairly high resistance to Dark Magic. She has been trying for a long time to resist the influence of Voldemort's horcrux.

Ginny became a Gryffindor hunter at the age of 14, temporarily replacing Harry in the team. She caught the snitch in all the matches described in the canon, although she flew on a far from the best broom. After graduating from Hogwarts, she played for Holyhead Harpies for several years.

Fred And George Weasley

Fred and George Weasley; April 1, 1978-twin brothers, sons of Arthur and Molly Weasley. They are known for their sense of humor. Wonderful beaters in the Gryffindor Quidditch team, Fred and George always stick together, so they usually don't talk about them separately. It is very difficult to distinguish them, which they use to play a prank around with others.

Character

Fred is a very active and impulsive person. Sometimes, even a twin brother can't cool his ardor. If you carefully read the book, it becomes clear that Fred is the ringleader and initiator of almost all the pranks. George just picks up on the idea. Fred is also more outgoing and brash compared to his brother, probably because George is shyer. Fred was cruel enough, he could blow up a salamander for fun or send Montague to a broken Vanishing Cabinet, which almost killed the Slytherin.

Nevertheless, Fred, like his brother, is always ready to come to the rescue and is kind to his friends and family. He is determined and brave and is always ready to stand up for himself and for his truth. Fred always tries to make people laugh, even in dark times. He does not like to make plans, he prefers improvisation and quickly navigates various situations. He and his brother are brilliant magicians, very talented and savvy, which has always helped them in life.

Like his twin brother, George is characterized by carelessness and frivolity and can amuse others with his jokes and practical jokes. George is more assiduous than his brother. One of the memorable traits of the younger twin's character is the ability to enjoy small things, which is proved by the case that occurred during the operation "Seven Potters." Even though George lost his ear, he found a way to console his mother, claiming that now she would be able to distinguish him from his brother.

Abilities

Fred and George, although not excellent students, are very capable and talented guys. They grasp on the fly the spells that Harry teaches them and pass the Apparition exam perfectly the first time. Professor Flitwick, a Spell instructor at Hogwarts, described Fred and George Portable Swamp as "exemplary witchcraft," according to Ginny.

By their nature, the brothers are inventors. It's not for nothing that the brothers create a lot of unique things for their magic jokes store themselves. To do this, they come up with various spells, potions, and much more. What is worth only their Headless Hat, which Hermione calls an unsurpassed level of magic.

Differences between the movies and books

The book twins have blue eyes, while the Phelps twins, who play their role in the films, have brown eyes. In the book, they are described as being stocky and shorter than their brother Ron, but in the film, they are slender and significantly taller than the actor who played Ron.

Neville Longbottom

Neville Longbottom is one of the key characters. He studied at Hogwarts School at the Gryffindor faculty in the same course as Harry Potter. In the first years, he was quite absent-minded, forgetful and awkward. Of all the disciplines studied at Hogwarts, he excelled most in Herbology. Subsequently, he became a professor at Hogwarts on this subject.

Orphan with living parents

Neville's parents are former aurors, members of the first Order of the Phoenix. After Voldemort disappeared, they fell into the hands of the Death Eaters. Bellatrix Lestrange and three like-minded people tortured them with the Cruciatus spell until they went mad. Since that time, Frank and Alice Longbottom have been in St. Mungo's Hospital. Neville lived with his grandmother and visited his parents but was shy to talk about them.

Living with his grandmother, Augusta Longbottom, for a long time, Neville did not demonstrate any magical abilities common to children of his age. For this reason, his relatives considered him Squib, and Algie's great-uncle repeatedly tried to scare him and thus provoke the manifestation of magic. Once, he almost drowned him, pushing him off the pier. In the first book, Neville, having met his future classmates, told about another similar case: "When I was eight, Algy came to our house for tea, caught me and stuck me out the window. I was hanging there upside down, and he was holding my ankles. And then my cousin Enid offered him a cake, and he accidentally unclenched his hands. I fell from the second floor, but I didn't crash — it was like I turned into a ball, bounced off the ground and jumped down the path. They were all delighted, and my grandmother even burst into tears with happiness." Be that as it may, the relatives were happy when Neville received a letter of admission to Hogwarts.

Other Students Of The Gryffindor Faculty

Lavender Brown. A classmate of Harry Potter. Purebred. She is known for her relationship with Ron Weasley in the sixth book. In the films, her role is played by Jesse Cave. Patronus - a canary.

Percy Ignatius Weasley. The third child in the Weasley family. Since the first book, he has been the head of the Gryffindor faculty at Hogwarts, studying in the fifth year. Patronus - parrot.

Seamus Finnigan. A fellow student of Harry Potter. Half-breed. In the fifth book, during the confrontation between the versions of Dumbledore and the Ministry about the revival of Voldemort, he takes the side of the Ministry, but after the "terror," Umbridge takes Harry's side. In films, the character often sets off small explosions, which are not consistent with the events of the books. The role of Seamus in the movie is played by Devon Murray. Patronus - fox.

Dean Thomas. A classmate of Harry Potter. A half-breed. In the fifth book, in the "information war", he takes Dumbledore's side. In the sixth book, he begins dating Ginny Weasley. The role of Dean in the films is played by Alfred Enoch. Patronus-wild boar.

Oliver Wood. The student is four years older than Harry. Thoroughbred. The captain and keeper of the Gryffindor Quidditch team in the first three books. He is passionate about this sport. After graduating from Hogwarts, he continues his sports career. He is credited to the second roster of Puddlemere United. He tells his former classmates about this when they all come together at the

Quidditch World Cup. In the films, the role of Oliver Wood is played by Sean Biggerstaff.

Katie Bell. A student a year older than Harry Potter, Chaser of the Gryffindor Quidditch Team. In the first five films, Katie is played by Emily Dale, in the following - Georgina Leonidas.

Lee Jordan. Sports commentator of Quidditch matches at Hogwarts. During matches, he often joked, trying to "enliven" his comments in an interesting way, so Professor McGonagall always sat next to him at matches. The best friend of the Weasley twins, together with them, wanted to get to the Triwizard Tournament. When Umbridge ruled at school, he launched Niffler to her office. During the terror of the Dark Lord, he hosted the Potterwatch radio program under the nickname River. Together with George Weasley, he defeated the Death Eater Corban Yaxley. In the film, he is played by Luke Youngblood.

Angelina Johnson. Chaser from the Quidditch team of the Gryffindor faculty, also captain of the team following the graduation of Oliver Wood. A half-breed. The same age as Fred and George. She went to the Yule Ball in the fourth book, accompanied by Fred Weasley. Later, she marries George Weasley and gives birth to a son and a daughter. In the films, the role of Angelina is played by Daniel Tabor and Tiana Benjamin.

Cormac McLaggen. The student is a year older than Harry Potter. Purebred. In the book "Harry Potter and the Half-Blood Prince," he took part in the selection of the Gryffindor Quidditch team for the role of Keeper. However, thanks to Hermione Granger, who disoriented him with a Confundus spell, Ron Weasley got a place in the team instead of him. Before the second game of Gryffindor, when the poisoned Ron went out of order, Harry Potter had to take Cormac into the team. McLaggen turned out to be arrogant. He began to give advice to other players, while playing worse. And when Harry made a remark to him, Cormac knocked Harry off the broom with a bludger, after which he was excluded from the team. His role in the films is played by Freddie Stroma.

Colin Creevey. A student a year younger than Harry Potter. A Muggle-born wizard. He is known from the second book, where he walks most of the time with a Muggle camera. He has a brother, Dennis Creevey, who is two years younger than him and is also enrolled in Gryffindor. Creevey is the only Muggle family known from Rowling's books, where two children are wizards at once. His role in the films is played by Hugh Mitchell.

Romilda Vane. A student two years younger than Harry. Purebred. She is known as the girl who unsuccessfully tried to attract Harry's attention in the sixth book. Once, she tried to slip Harry Potter candy with love potion, which Ron Weasley ate instead of a potential victim. Her role in the films is played by Anna Shaffer.

2. SLYTHERIN STUDENTS

Draco Malfoy

Draco Lucius Malfoy is a pure-blooded wizard, a student of Hogwarts, the same age as Harry Potter. For many reasons, the boys became sworn enemies even in their first year. He studied at the Slytherin faculty, like many of his relatives before him. Being the son of the Death Eater Lucius Malfoy, Draco completely adopted his militant attitude towards Muggles, becoming an adherent of the pureblood doctrine. He is quite smart, active, ambitious.

Appearance

Draco is tall and thin, with smooth blond hair, a pointed face, cold gray eyes, pale skin, thin features and a sharp nose. He is aristocratic and important because he considers himself above others because of the status of blood. When he is confused or angry, pink spots appear on his pale cheeks. He has a habit of mannerly stretching words.

Character traits

Draco Malfoy has a complex character in which both positive and negative qualities are mixed. In addition, the boy is growing, and with this growth, some features of his nature appear more clearly, while others, on the contrary, fade away. Very clearly, the character of the young Malfoy appeared twice: when meeting Harry Potter in Madame Malkin's Store and in an attempt to continue this acquaintance in the Hogwarts Express. He is arrogant, ambitious, portrays himself as a "tough guy," and mentally has not yet developed.

Gradually, life teaches Draco lesson after lesson, which he does not learn at first. It is very difficult for a spoiled scion of an ancient aristocratic family to understand that neither great wealth, nor high social status, nor even great meanness can make you a winner, give you power over the world and people, even just give you what you want. Sometimes, you need to change yourself to do this. And Draco is changing, however, very slowly. Sometimes, when his actions are knocked out of the image of a "high-born pure-blooded wizard-aristocrat," Draco has a complex and begins to prove to everyone around that it was an unfortunate accident. He clings for a long time and stubbornly to the qualities that were instilled in him in the family.

Malfoy was lucky to meet Harry Potter at the very beginning of his school years. A mental comparison with this friend-enemy for six years makes Draco mentally develop. Perhaps, this comparison reached its peak in the fifth year, when Draco becomes both the head of the faculty and the favorite of the new director, gets power over all the students of Hogwarts (the status of a member of the Inquisitorial Squad gave many privileges), wins the favor of Minister Fudge, and he feels supported not only by the power of his father but also by the shadow of Voldemort's power. And Harry, who has none of this, comes out victorious again. In addition, Draco, who had soared so high, had to fall painfully at the end of the year: Umbridge was dismissed from Hogwarts, Fudge was dismissed from the post of minister, his father was put in Azkaban, and such drastic changes always give food for thought.

The subsequent entry into the ranks of the Death Eaters, the task given by the Dark Lord, the real danger hanging over the Malfoy family if this task is not completed finally pulls Draco out of his childhood and force him to rethink a lot of things. No wonder a year later-it's a completely different Draco. And now Harry, who has learned all these "life lessons" for a long time, sincerely sympathizes with Malfoy, understanding what choice the Owner put the young man before.

Draco's bad character is largely not his fault but the result of erroneous principles of upbringing in his family. However, to be honest, a huge plus of the Malfoy family is that they really love each other. The fear that something terrible could happen to him and his family is enough motivation for Draco.

Skills and abilities

Malfoy flies well on a broomstick and was a member of the Slytherin Quidditch team. Draco studies well, especially succeeds in the lessons on Defense against the Dark Art (DADA) and Potions. Also, Malfoy owns Occlumency at a fairly high level. This skill is perfectly consistent with the character of Draco. It was easy for him to "turn off" emotions, cut off and reject important parts of himself, which is necessary for Occlumency.

At the end of the fifth book, Dumbledore tells Harry that the fact that he can feel such pain is an integral part of his humanity; with Draco, the opposite is true — this is a clear example that denying pain and suppressing internal conflict can only lead to the destruction of the personality (which is more likely than harming others).

Behind the scenes

1. In the film, the role of Draco Malfoy is played by Tom Felton, who, according to some sources, auditioned for the role of the main character — Harry Potter, as well as for the role of Ron Weasley but failed to pass the audition for these roles.

2. Especially for the role, Tom Felton's hair was bleached almost to white.

3. The performer of the role of Draco Malfoy, actor Tom Felton, was one of the few children on the set who already had professional acting experience behind them.

4. Draco Malfoy's wand is one of the few whose design has not changed throughout the Harry

Potter films.

5. In the first two films, Tom Felton's hair was carefully slicked back, but this was extremely inconvenient for both the actor and the make-up artists, so from the third film, Draco's hair acquired a more "urban style" (according to the director).

6. J. K. Rowling considers Draco Malfoy a character of dubious morality. Therefore, she is very upset by the number of girls who "fell for" Malfoy. She suggests that this is partly because many girls tend to romanticize "bad guys."

Vincent Crabbe

Vincent Crabbe is a Slytherin, a classmate of Harry Potter, a friend of Draco Malfoy. However, "friend" is a strong word. For friendship with the younger Malfoy, Vincent does not have enough brains, nor character, nor an elementary position in society. Rather, he serves as Draco's bodyguard, a silent six, an errand boy. However, Malfoy knows how to be generous if it does not contradict his plans. Undoubtedly, it was he who insisted that the Beaters take Crabbe and Goyle (his second backup singer) to the faculty Quidditch team, where Draco was already a Seeker.

Crabbe studied very poorly, crawling over to the next course with great difficulty. He kicks someone in the corridor with Goyle until their teachers see them.

Crabbe's loyalty to Malfoy was unwavering, despite the constant troubles and punishments caused by the Draco-Potter confrontation. In the sixth year, Malfoy became withdrawn and began hiding in the Rescue Room, leaving Vincent and Goyle on guard at the door.

Appearance

Vincent is a big, early-stretched boy and has amazing high-pitched voice sounds. Harry noted that his neck was thicker than the body of a freshman, Colin Creevey. Crabbe never swings his arms when walking, as if they are stuck to his body.

Gregory Goyle

Gregory Goyle, like Vincent Crabb — is Draco Malfoy's best friend (if, of course, Draco has any friends at all). Harry Potter calls Crabbe and Goyle "bodyguards" of Malfoy. Born into a family of pure-blooded wizards, Gregory was the son of a Death Eater, especially close to Voldemort. Throughout the novel, it can be noticed that neither the father nor the son of Goyle are distinguished by a special mind.

Pansy Parkinson

Pansy Parkinson is a Slytherin student, the same age as Harry Potter. She is snub-nosed and has a low stature. Harry and Hermione, who do not like Slytherins, call her a cow or a pug behind her back. Even in the first book, Rowling herself refers to Pansy as "a girl from Slytherin with rough facial features."

Biography facts

Pansy entered Hogwarts in 1991 and was selected for the Slytherin faculty. Quite early, she falls under the influence of her classmate Draco Malfoy. She does a lot of things imitating Draco; at least, she teases the Gryffindors and Harry Potter, in particular. Subsequently, her attachment to Malfoy grows into something more, but she never achieves reciprocity.

Pansy is a very active person; in the fifth year, she was chosen as the head of the faculty and also joined the Inquisitorial Squad. Apparently, she was too active: someone conjured her horns in revenge, and the girl had to spend several days in the hospital wing.

In an interview, Rowling said that Pansy is one of her least favorite characters because she contains all those prototypes of arrogant and haughty girls that the writer herself had to face in her young years.

Other Students Of The Slytherin Faculty

Millicent Bulstrode is a student of the Slytherin faculty, the same age as Harry Potter and a classmate of Draco Malfoy. She is characterized by a dense build and a heavy jaw. In the dueling club, she participated in a duel with Hermione, and then Hermione used her hair for Polyjuice Potion, but the hair turned out to be a cat's.

Marcus Flint is a Slytherin student, the captain of the faculty Quidditch team. He accepted Draco Malfoy into the team in the second book. Marcus was described as tall and relatively muscular. He had big teeth, shifty gray eyes, and coarse black hair. He reminded Harry Potter of a troll.

3. RAVENCLAW STUDENTS

Luna Lovegood

Luna Lovegood is a student at Hogwarts and studied at the Ravenclaw Faculty a year younger than Harry Potter. Luna's father, Xenophilius, is the publisher of The Quibbler magazine.

The students of Hogwarts consider Luna a little crazy and shun her. It seems that with the exception of Harry Potter and his company, she has no friends, and even with those, the rapprochement did not happen immediately. Harry and Neville are puzzled by Luna, she makes Hermione mad, Ginny sometimes can hardly contain her laughter in her presence, and Ron calls her crazy in general openly. The guys were able to truly appreciate the peculiar girl with "radishes in her ears" only after the Battle in the Department of Mysteries.

As is often the case in schools, Luna, due to her strange character, appearance and beliefs, becomes a victim of bullying from her classmates. They call her "Loony Lovegood," steal her things, taunt her appearance. Nevertheless, Luna is not angry with them; on the contrary, she forgives her offenders with kindness. Apparently, having lost your mother at the age of nine, you begin to understand that there are more serious and more important things in life than hidden shoes.

Appearance

Luna Lovegood looks quite unusual. She has "large clouded eyes," which is repeatedly emphasized in the text of the books — "bulging, as if slightly clouded eyes," "pale eyebrows and bulging eyes all the time gave her a surprised look."

Luna dresses very extravagantly.

Characteristics and abilities

For all her eccentricity and adherence to strange beliefs, Luna is quite an intelligent and capable sorceress. She is quite successfully trained in defense magic at Dumbledore's Army classes and participates in a fight with Death Eaters at the Ministry of Magic. In this battle, she shows no less courage than the Gryffindors and is extremely cold-blooded at the same time; sometimes, it seems that she is completely devoid of fear. She manages to save and pull out of the fight both Ginny with a broken leg, and Ron, who was stunned by the spell. It seems to some researchers that Sorting Hat made a rare mistake.

Also, do not forget that she is studying at the faculty of Ravenclaw, where only smart students get. Thanks to her uninhibited thinking, she sometimes manages to find the most unexpected solutions. In the fifth book, she guesses to use thestrals to get to London; in the seventh book, that the object that Harry is looking for may be the diadem of Rowena Ravenclaw.

Other Students Of The Ravenclaw Faculty

Cho Chang. A student older than Harry by a year. The patronus - swan. She first appears in the book "Harry Potter and the Prisoner of Azkaban": she is the Seeker of the Ravenclaw team. At the Ravenclaw - Gryffindor match, she is noticed (and noted) by Harry Potter. Gradually Harry falls in love with her but hesitates to approach her. Cho meets with Cedric Diggory for a while. In the book "Harry Potter and the Order of the Phoenix," after the death of Cedric Diggory, the relationship between Zhou and Harry reaches its climax. However, Zhou is very worried: it seems to her that by meeting Harry, she is cheating on Cedric's memory. This was one of the reasons for the breakup of their relationship in the same book. Since self-doubt and guilt make Zhou tearful, which, in turn, begins to annoy Harry, and her gratuitous, as it seems to him, jealousy of Hermione puts him at a dead end.

Zhou is attractive and contentedly sweet but has a complex, unstable character. She is quite emotional and often cries.

She was a member of Dumbledore's Army. The role of Zhou in the films is played by Kathy Leung.

Michael Corner. Harry's classmate. A half-breed. He is best known as Ginny Weasley's first boyfriend. Because of his relationship with Ginny, he was drawn into Dumbledore's Army by her. He received the highest score for OWLs in Potions and was one of the few of Harry's peers accepted into the Horace Slughorn class. Ginny broke up with Michael because of his dissatisfaction with the victory of Gryffindor in Quidditch. Michael started dating Cho Chang. In the seventh book, Neville Longbottom says that Michael Corner was tortured by Alecto and Amycus Carrow for trying to save freshmen from prison. He was also one of several members of Dumbledore's Army who insisted on their participation in the Battle for Hogwarts.

Marietta Edgecombe. Ravenclaw student, one of Cho Chang's friends. Blonde with curly hair. Marietta joined Dumbledore's Squad under pressure from a group gathered at Hog's Head Inn. Marietta later betrayed Dumbledore's Army to Umbridge, but the parchment on which all the members of the squad signed at the first meeting was enchanted by Hermione, and pimples appeared on Marietta's face, folding into the word "sneak." Umbridge arranged a confrontation between Harry and Marietta so that she would confirm the fact of classes in the Room of Requirement, but Kingsley Shacklebolt slightly changed her memory to save Harry and his friends from problems. Marietta's betrayal put an end to the relationship between Harry and Zhou, as she began to justify friend. In the sixth book, Marietta still has the effects of Hermione's spell. In the film, instead of Marietta, who voluntarily betrayed Dumbledore's Army, the secret was revealed by Zhou Chang under the influence of Veritaserum.

4. HUFFLEPUFF STUDENTS

Cedric Diggory

Cedric Diggory is a student of Hufflepuff. Three years older than Harry Potter, he is one of the main characters of the fourth part. The only child of Amos Diggory and his wife, Cedric Diggory is described as a "strong but quiet type," "terribly attractive," honest and brave. He was the captain and Seeker of the Hufflepuff Quidditch team, the head of the faculty and, in general, an excellent student. In 1994, he turned 17 years old; that is, he was born in 1977, but in the same 1994, Cedric is only in the sixth year, which means he entered Hogwarts in 1989. Cedric's father, Amos Diggory, works in the Department for the Regulation and Control of Magical Creatures at the Ministry of Magic.

Biography

Cedric first appears in the third book as the captain of the Hufflepuff team. Diggory catches the snitch a little earlier than Harry in the Hufflepuff-Gryffindor match, but after learning that at the last moment, Harry fainted and fell off his broom at the appearance of dementors on the field, he offers to replay the match. The captain of the Gryffindor team, Oliver Wood, refused this offer and admitted that the Hufflepuff won fairly (the score was 150: 50 in favor of Hufflepuff).

We learn a little more about Cedric when father and son Diggory, who, it turns out, lives near The Burrow, near the village of Ottery St Catchpole, together with the Weasley family, Harry Potter and Hermione Granger, go through the portal to the Quidditch World Cup. It is noteworthy that Cedric was very embarrassed for his father's boastful statement that the younger Diggory "defeated Harry Potter."

In October 1994, the Triwizard Tournament, revived after a centuries-long break, opened at Hogwarts. Representatives of two more magic schools came to the Tournament: Beauxbatons and Durmstrang. Diggory was chosen by the Goblet of Fire as the champion from Hogwarts. The faculty of Hufflepuff, not spoiled by awards, was in seventh heaven with happiness...

Appearance

Cedric is an attractive young man. It wasn't just Zhou Chang who had her eye on him. Gryffindor girls of senior courses also note that Cedric is "laconic and good-looking" (however, Oliver Wood says that Diggory "can't connect two words, so he is silent"). Even Frenchwoman Fleur Delacour tries to charm Diggory with her Veela charms. True, it gets into Ron Weasley.

Magical abilities

Gifted - Cedric surpassed his peers in magical abilities. In the 6th year, after using the portal, he alone managed to resist on his feet together with the adults, while all the other children (including his classmates, the Weasley twins) crashed into the ground with all their might.

Transfiguration - Cedric was a good specialist in this field and managed to transform a stone into a dog during the First test. In the 4th year, he turned the whistle into a clock, and they told the time (according to Professor Moody).

Charms - Cedric was just as good a specialist. He managed to conjure a breathing bubble on the Second test.

Quidditch - Cedric was a good Quidditch player.

Behind the scenes

1. In Harry Potter and the Goblet of Fire, Robert Pattinson portrays Cedric Diggory.

2. Robert Pattinson admitted that he enjoyed playing Cedric in Harry Potter more than Edward Cullen in Twilight.

Other Students Of The Hufflepuff Faculty

Justin Finch-Fletchley. The same age as Harry Potter. Muggle-born. In his sophomore year, during the first and last training session of the Dueling Club, he decided that Harry Potter was inciting a snake at him when Harry, unknowingly, demonstrated the Parseltongue's abilities (in fact, Harry shouted to the snake: "Get out!"). Soon, he was attacked by a basilisk but survived thanks to the fact that he looked at him through Nearly Headless Nick. Revived by the Mandrake potion, in the fifth year, he joined Dumbledore's Army. Together with other members of Dumbledore's Army, he saved Harry Potter from Malfoy, Crabbe and Goyle on the train and participated in the Battle of Hogwarts. The character was played by Edward Randall.

Ernest Macmillan. The same age as Harry Potter. A pure-blooded wizard. In the second book, Ernie believes that Harry is the heir of Slytherin and convinces his classmates of this, trying in every possible way to catch Potter in a crime. But when Hermione was attacked, he admits that it wasn't him and apologizes. Since then, Harry and Ernie have become friends, but in the fourth book, Ernie, like the whole school, considers Potter a fraud who wanted to snatch Cedric's fame. In the fifth book, he publicly says that he believes Harry Potter that Voldemort has been reborn.

Ernie is a bit pompous and likes to express himself in a florid way, but he studies well and always stands for truth and justice.

He joins Dumbledore's Army And becomes the headman of the Hufflepuff. Together with Luna and Seamus, he saves Harry, Ron and Hermione from dementors. The patronus - boar. The character was played by Louis Doyle andJamie Marks.

Zacharias Smith. Member of Dumbledore's Army and a Quidditch player on the Hufflepuff team. Of all the members of Dumbledore's Army, one always treats Harry badly. Even at the first meeting in the bar, Hog's Head Inn shows his disbelief in the rebirth of the Dark Lord. He doesn't believe in the effectiveness of the disarming charm. At one of the games, he acts as a commentator, where he criticizes Potter's team in every possible way, and at the end of the game, Ginny rams the commentator's platform on a broomstick, throwing Smith to the ground. During the Battle of Hogwarts, he escapes even before the battle begins: Harry sees Zacharias trying to fight his way to the exit, pushing the freshmen aside. The character was played by Nick Shirm.

People find it far easier to forgive others for being wrong than being right.

— Albus Dumbledore

HP Quotes

5. TEACHERS AND STAFF

Albus Dumbledore

Albus Percival Wulfric Brian Dumbledore is one of the main characters in the Harry Potter novels, Professor of Transfiguration, Director of the Hogwarts School of Witchcraft and Wizardry, Knight of the Order of Merlin First Degree, Grand Sorcerer, Chief Warlock Wizengamot, head of the International Confederation of Wizards. Known as the strongest wizard of his time.

Achievements, awards, notes

- Dumbledore is also famous as an alchemist, who, in his youth, attracted the attention of Nicolas Flamel, the famous creator of the Philosopher's Stone. At one time, they worked together to create new potions, and the bonds of friendship bound them until their death.

- Dumbledore discovered twelve ways to use dragon's blood.

- In 1945, at the age of 64, Albus Dumbledore defeated Gellert Grindelwald, a dark wizard whom he had not met since that memorable day of Ariana's death. As a result, he becomes the master of Elder Wand.

- By the time he graduated from Hogwarts, Dumbledore was already the winner of the Barnabus Finkley Prize for outstanding success in casting spells and was awarded a Gold Medal for his landmark performance at the International Alchemical Conference in Cairo. Later, the Order of Merlin of the first degree was added to his awards (apparently, for the victory over Gellert Grindelwald).

- His Patronus took the form of a phoenix.

- His boggart, as Rowling herself said on one of the forums, is the corpse of his sister. She also said that if Dumbledore had looked in the Mirror of Erised, he would have seen all his family members alive and happy.

Appearance

Dumbledore is described as a tall, thin and very old man with silver hair and a beard (both were so long that he could easily have tucked them into his belt). His blue eyes shone brightly from under half-moon glasses that sat on a long nose so hooked that it looked as if it had been broken at least twice. According to his own words, there is a scar above his left knee that exactly matches the scheme of the London underground.

Skills and character

Albus Dumbledore looked like a gray-haired sage, understanding everything, forgiving everything... Nevertheless, despite his external good nature, a certain extravagance and eccentricity, he was considered the most powerful wizard of his time. In his rage, he was very scary — his eyes no longer sparkled with lights, and his glasses did not sparkle conspiratorially — he radiated such power that you could feel it physically, and this made it creepy. No wonder Dumbledore was the only one Lord Voldemort was afraid of.

He often puts the names of his favorite sweets as a password to enter his office. For example, his passion is Sherbet lemon. The only thing he doesn't like is Bertie Bott's Every Flavor Beans: in his youth, he came across a candy with the taste of vomit. He admitted that he loves Muggle knitting patterns and that no one has ever given him wool socks.

He constantly demonstrates his extraordinary talent as a wizard. He combines his magical abilities with dexterity and ingenuity and with such human qualities as trust, love and friendship, which puts Voldemort in a difficult position.

Kindness and trust

Dumbledore believes that there is good in every person, only sometimes it is very deeply hidden. It happens that only faith in a person awakens in him his best qualities. For example, after the repentance of Severus Snape, who had previously been a Death Eater, Dumbledore completely trusted him and entrusted him with important tasks. And this is despite the bad character of Snape and the fact that none of Dumbledore's associates completely trusted Snape.

However, do not consider the headmaster of Hogwarts a gullible simpleton! He is an excellent judge of who is trustworthy and who is just trying to ingratiate himself into trust.

Magic Power

Dumbledore developed a method of sending messages through the Patronus and taught this skill to the members of the Order of the Phoenix. He has the ability to become invisible without using the Invisibility cloak, has Occlumency and Legilimency, is able to cast magic without a wand and is perfectly proficient in the non-verbal method of casting spells. He is also a master of combat spells and apparition.

Minerva Mcgonagall

Minerva McGonagall, Deputy Headmaster of the Hogwarts School of Witchcraft and Wizardry, Dean of Gryffindor, Transfiguration teacher, later Headmaster of Hogwarts.

Professor McGonagall is not only an experienced teacher (she has been working at Hogwarts since December 1956) but also a powerful sorceress. For example, she is a registered Animagus, i.e., she can take the form of an animal, namely a striped cat with markings around the eyes.

Appearance

A tall, rather stern-looking woman with dark, sometimes gray hair gathered in a strict bun, wearing square glasses of the same shape as the markings around the eyes of the cat she was turning into.

Character traits

In the seventh chapter of the first book, McGonagall meets first-year students, including Harry Potter. The main character immediately comes to mind that it is better not to contradict this lady. However, this impression is only half true. Professor McGonagall is really strict and principled, but nothing human is alien to her. For example, when Harry climbed on a broomstick and flew into the air without the teacher's permission at his first broom flying lesson, instead of punishing the boy, McGonagall invited him to the Gryffindor Quidditch team. Minerva is not a pedant or a dogmatist. She is well aware that there are circumstances that cancel some rules. So, she did not scold Harry for using the Unforgivable Curse Cruciatus to Amycus Carrow, and five minutes later, she herself cast an Imperius spell on the hated Devourer. Apparently, she rightly believes that the struggle has entered the stage when lives are at stake...

The image of McGonagall is revealed especially vividly in a verbal altercation with Senior Undersecretary of Magic and Hogwarts High Inquisitor Dolores Umbridge. This is one of the most striking episodes of the book. The essence of the conflict lies in the fact that the Minister for Magic refuses to recognize the revival of the Dark Lord Voldemort. Moreover, Minister Cornelius Fudge considers all of Dumbledore's claims about the return of He Who Must Not Be Named a political intrigue aimed at overthrowing Fudge. Therefore, Umbridge is being given more and more powers at Hogwarts. She is interfering more and more unceremoniously in the educational process, trying to limit the activities of teachers who sympathize with the director.

This confrontation looks especially original if we consider it at the level of Patronuses: two Cats hiss at each other because of the territory.

To fight Voldemort, Dumbledore once again assembled a special organization — the Order of the Phoenix, of which McGonagall herself is a member. The Order performed well during the First Wizarding War, but because of the position of the Ministry, it is now forced to act underground.

When Umbridge and her henchmen got the long-awaited reason to arrest Dumbledore as a troublemaker and a rebel, McGonagall expressed her willingness to fight on the side of the headmaster. Dumbledore persuaded her not to do this: "Do not interfere — Hogwarts needs you." He managed to avoid arrest and leave the school, after which Umbridge took over his post. During the period of Umbridge's stay in power, McGonagall withdrew from assisting the new director in every possible way: she did not even think to fight the magical fireworks organized by the Weasley twins, ignored Umbridge's recommendations about Harry Potter, and even gave advice to the poltergeist Peeves about how best to unscrew the chandelier (Peeves wanted to drop it on someone's unlucky head). At the consultation on choosing a future profession, despite Umbridge's objections, McGonagall said that she would help Harry become an Auror, if necessary — she would teach him at night and make sure that he achieved the necessary results.

McGonagall stood up for Hagrid when the Ministry staff came for him and was stunned by them, after which she was sent to St Mungo's Hospital. Madam Pomfrey (the school healer) commented on this: "If only one of them would try to defeat Minerva McGonagall in broad daylight, meeting her face to face! Cowardice, that's what it is... the most despicable cowardice!"

Apparently, McGonagall is originally from Scotland. This is evidenced by the following facts: her last name; the fact that she appeared at the Yule Ball in a red tartan mantle and with a wreath of thistles (a traditional symbol of Scotland), offered Harry ginger cookies (familiar to Scottish cuisine) from a jar with a checkered pattern, wears a tartan robe and uses a checkered handkerchief.

In one of his dreams, Harry Potter saw McGonagall playing the bagpipes. And the bagpipe is a traditional Scottish musical instrument.

Magic Power

Minerva's patronus is a cat. At the same time, she can cause several patronuses at once. McGonagall is an unsurpassed master of Transfiguration and Apparition. She knows a lot of combat spells and is able to control the protective charms of Hogwarts, even without being the headmaster of the school.

Interesting facts

Professor McGonagall is the first wizard introduced in the Harry Potter series of books and appears in the first chapter of the first book in her Animagus shape. However, in the films, McGonagall is a second wizard and a character since Albus Dumbledore appears before her. She is the second character introduced in the film and the first woman introduced in the film.

The name Minerva is borrowed from the Roman goddess of wisdom, the patroness of warriors.

Severus Snape

Severus Snape is the most controversial character in the saga. Lecturer in Potions (1981-1996) and Defense against the Dark Art (1996-1997), Dean of the Slytherin Faculty from 1981-1997, and later, Director of the Hogwarts School of Witchcraft and Wizardry from 1997-1998.

Appearance

Snape was a thin man with pale skin, a hooked nose and greasy, shoulder-length hair. His cold, black eyes resembled "dark tunnels," the same black as Hagrid's, but they did not have the warmth that shone in the giant's eyes. Snape was of medium height, with thin lips, which often wore a mocking smile. He spoke in a soft, low voice, which, however, had a steel note. He could silence a noisy class in a low whisper.

Snape preferred to wear a black robe fluttering in the wind, which made him look like a bat. In general, Snape barely paid attention to his appearance. His always greasy, unwashed hair was the subject of ridicule and jokes. According to Rowling, he attached more importance to his inner world than to how he looked.

Magic skills

Snape is not a light wizard, but he was not a dark wizard. He invented spells, at least one of which could easily kill a person. He knew how to summon a corporeal Patronus.

1. An outstanding potion maker, he improved the composition and preparation of potions.

2. Possessed a talent at Occlumency.

3. Creator of new spells.

4. A wizard who knew how to move through the air without any vehicle (except for Snape, only Voldemort demonstrated this skill).

5. Possesses the Legilimency skill.

Non-magical abilities

1. A person who had clear logical thinking (few wizards can boast of this).

2. Prudent strategist, skillful tactician.

3. A person who could perfectly hide his feelings, if necessary, for the case.

4. Not a bad psychologist. At least finding a "pain point" of the interlocutor for Snape does not seem particularly difficult.

Relationship with Harry Potter

With Harry, Snape is connected, perhaps, by the most complex and contradictory relationships. On the one hand, the protection of the boy is a kind of tribute to the memory of the deceased Lily. And Severus does not forget for a second about the one for whom the beloved woman gave her life. But at the same time, Harry is an indirect cause of her death. This duality of perception of the younger Potter intensified when Snape saw how similar the boy was to his father, the hated James, who took Lily away from Severus and failed to protect her.

Throughout all six years of training, Snape gets quite a distinct pleasure from all sorts of nasty things and jokes that he says to Harry (something that he could not or could not afford to address James). However, in the depths of his soul, the professor gradually gets more and more warm feelings for the boy. From the first year of meeting Potter, Snape does not hesitate for a moment to protect Harry's life and health in any situation. Harry does not notice the striking contradiction between what Professor Snape says and what he does, and the further away, the more brazenly he responds to Snape's attacks. From "But it seems to me that Hermione knows this for sure, why don't you ask her?" in the first year, to a completely boorish phrase: "You don't have to call me 'sir', Professor" on the sixth.

And yet, when Snape finds out that Albus Dumbledore is ready to sacrifice Harry in the fight against Voldemort, he is genuinely shocked. It turns out that the boy had been kept alive only up to a certain point in order to give him "like a pig for slaughter"! And when the sagacious Dumbledore asks if Snape has become attached to the boy, Severus hides behind only the memory of Lily. He seems to be trying to hide it even from himself, but he really values Harry.

The most ambiguous character

Who Severus is really devoted to remains a mystery (at least for Harry and his friends) until the death of the Potion Master during the Battle for Hogwarts. A few minutes before his death, Snape manages to give his memories to Harry Potter. After reviewing them, the young man is convinced that the man whom he hated and considered the murderer of the previous director was actually acting on the orders of Dumbledore himself and was playing a dangerous game against Voldemort. It was he who told Dumbledore about the Dark Lord's plans to kill the Potter family, it was he who looked after Harry from the very beginning, protecting him, it was he who suggested the idea of the seven Potters to Mundungus Fletcher, it was he who, remaining unrecognized, gave Harry the sword of Gryffindor. Even the most terrible crime that Harry blamed on Snape, the death of Professor Dumbledore, was not murder per se. It turns out that the director, who is near death, asked, begged, insisted that it was Severus who killed him and not the sixteen-year-old Draco Malfoy, whose soul the old professor tried to protect from the irreparable.

But the greatness of this fearless man was revealed to Harry Potter too late. The only way a young man can repay his deceased teacher is to whitewash his honest name in the eyes of the magical community. And he fulfilled this duty. It was Harry who made sure that the portrait of Professor

Snape hung in the office of the headmaster of Hogwarts, as well as the portraits of the other deceased headmasters of the school.

Severus Snape in the fan subculture

Since some fans consider Snape to be the most ambiguous and interesting character in the Harry Potter series of books, he has a lot of fans. Fans themselves largely attribute this to the performance of the role of Snape by actor Alan Rickman. Snape fans write fan fiction, articles and research about Snape, exchange drawings and photos related to the character. This phenomenon is called "Snapemania."

Rubeus Hagrid

Rubeus Hagrid is a teacher of Care of Magical Creatures and Keeper of Keys and Grounds at the Hogwarts School of Witchcraft and Wizardry. Everyone just calls him Hagrid.

Origin

Hagrid is half human, half giant (he's at least 11 feet tall). His mother, the giantess Fridwulfa, left his father when Rubeus was still a child. Hagrid has a half-brother, a giant, whose name is Grawp, whom Hagrid tried to teach English. Giants have a reputation for being huge and stupid killers, who, moreover, were on the side of Lord Voldemort in the First Wizarding War, so Hagrid keeps his origin a secret.

Personality

Hagrid is good-natured, patient, attentive and vulnerable. He has a great love for animals, is ready to see a cute pet in every monster, so he manages to tame even the most ferocious of them. Some people think that he is unsociable, clumsy, ignorant... But this is not so. If Hagrid makes friends with someone, then you will not find a more loyal friend. He has a special warmth for Harry Potter and his friends and was always glad to see them at his house.

Also, Hagrid is not ambitious and does not try to make enemies. He works as a forester, and he is quite satisfied with this. Even after he was reinstated in the rights to use magic, and Dumbledore accepted him as a professor of caring for magical creatures, Hagrid's life did not change much. He continued to live in his hut, take care of the Forbidden Forest and its inhabitants, and did not even part with his old broken wand. He taught classes with students in the open air and in accordance with his ideas about which animals are dangerous and which are not.

Interesting facts

1. He has some problems with spelling since, on the cake in the first film, he wrote not HAPPY, but HAPPEE, and BIRTHDAE instead of BIRTHDAY.

2. He often uses colloquial words, which adds uniqueness and imagery to his speech.

3. The blood of giants that flows in the veins of Rubeus makes him invulnerable to simple spells.

4. There is also information that a Polyjuice potion does not work on him because Rubeus is not in the full sense of a person.

5. Has an allergy to cats.

Filius Flitwick

Filius Flitwick - Professor of Charms at the Hogwarts School of Witchcraft and Wizardry, Dean of the Ravenclaw Faculty.

Filius Flitwick was born on October 17 in a family of wizards of goblin origin. At Hogwarts, he was assigned to the Ravenclaw faculty. After only five minutes of hesitation between Gryffindor and Ravenclaw, Sorting Hat sent him to the last one.

Work at Hogwarts

It is not known exactly when Flitwick got a job at Hogwarts, but, most likely, he has a very long experience. His teaching style is more "laid back" than his colleagues, such as Minerva McGonagall and Severus Snape. For example, he allowed students to play games in their classroom ahead of Christmas. However, this does not make him a bad teacher, which is confirmed by the words of George Weasley:" [...] everyone passes his exams well." Professor Flitwick has a great sense of humor and treats well not only students from Ravenclaw but also students from other faculties. He does not withdraw points even for being late for lessons. He also supported students who were experimenting with magic themselves and usually did not impose punishments on those who did not complete their homework; instead, he preferred to give them additional tasks so that they could catch up with the class.

Flitwick enjoys a well-deserved prestige among other professors and students, thanks to his knowledge and very non-conflicting nature.

Appearance

In all the released adaptations of Rowling's books, the role of Filius Flitwick is played by Warwick Davis. Despite this, the appearance of the professor in the first and second films is very different from his image in the subsequent pictures. Alfonso Cuaron, the director of the third film, did not leave Flitwick in the plot but introduced the choir conductor, and the director of the fourth film, Mike Newell, liked this image so much that he decided to combine Flitwick with the conductor. Thus, the appearance of Flitwick has changed a lot. From a gray-haired elderly wizard, he turned into a middle-aged conductor, and there was not a single scene of his lesson on the screens anymore (only a choir rehearsal in the film "Harry Potter and the Order of the Phoenix"). Therefore, the audience may have a wrong understanding of this character.

Personality

Professor Flitwick has goblins among his ancestors and is, therefore, very short in stature. However, his small stature is more than compensated for by his high magical knowledge and abilities. In addition, Flitwick is very kind in handling: he can even express his claims and criticism in such a form that formally, there will be nothing to be offended at.

Belonging to the faculty of Ravenclaw does not imply the presence of encyclopedic knowledge (although they are not superfluous) but a special mindset, unconventional thinking, the ability to find non-obvious analogies... And, apparently, the ability to avoid unpleasant situations in life, too. Flitwick corresponds to all these qualities as well as possible. In addition, he is very friendly to students, and they pay him back.

Magical abilities and skills

- **Duel**: At one time, Flitwick was the champion of the dueling club, which suggests that already at a young age, the future professor showed high magical abilities.

- **Charms**: As a charms master, Flitwick could create powerful shield spells and may have also invented several of his own spells.

- **Transfiguration**: The professor successfully uses Transfiguration skills when he creates Christmas decorations or makes part of the Portable Swamp disappear (he left a tiny piece in the corridor on purpose), which was created by the Weasley twins in protest against Umbridge's rule at Hogwarts.

- **Potions**: Gilderoy Lockhart claimed that Flitwick knows more about love spells than any wizard. Perhaps the professor once studied potions in depth.

Horace Slughorn

Horace Eugene Flaccus Slughorn is a pure-blood wizard, Potions Master and Dean of the Slytherin Faculty at the Hogwarts School of Witchcraft and Wizardry, an old friend of Albus Dumbledore. He worked at the school until his retirement in 1981.

In 1996, with Harry's help, Dumbledore persuades Slughorn to return to Hogwarts and start teaching. Before starting his studies, Slughorn, as he did in previous years, gathered a Slug Club consisting of the children of the most influential parents, celebrities and gifted students.

Later, it turns out that Slughorn's invitation to Hogwarts has a connection with the victory over Voldemort. Slughorn worked as a potions teacher during the years of Tom Riddle's studies there, who once started a conversation with the professor on a forbidden topic — about horcruxes. Dumbledore had a memory of this event, but it was corrected because Horace was ashamed of what had happened. However, Harry managed to convince Slughorn to pass on the real, not corrected memory. After that, Dumbledore finally established himself in the tasks of the struggle, having learned that in order to win, it is necessary to find and destroy six particles of the Dark Lord's soul.

After the escape of Severus Snape from Hogwarts, Slughorn was appointed by Professor McGonagall as the dean of Slytherin. He remained to teach at Hogwarts during the reign of Voldemort.

Appearance

In the book, Slughorn is a very fat, short old man with a bald head and a lush walrus mustache. In the film, he has no mustache and has quite decent hair, plus he is quite tall and dense but not fat.

Character traits

Horace Slughorn is an ambiguous figure. He is a little cowardly, but at the same time, he does not lose his head from fear. He will try to avoid danger, but at the same time, he will never agree to meanness in order to get rid of this danger. When faced with the dilemma of whether to live on the run or join the Death Eaters, Horace chose to flee. Professor Slughorn is very fond of comfortable, solid things, cozy furniture, fine wines and no less exquisite food. He perceives people primarily as a possible source of providing all sorts of rarities and delicacies. If at the same time, there is an opportunity to bask in the rays of someone else's glory, Slughorn will not miss this opportunity.

The old professor is well-versed in what can and cannot benefit him. He selects from his students the most capable, or the most punchy, or at least those who have influential relatives and acquaintances. Slughorn's flair for those who will go far is amazing. And at the same time, he is deeply indifferent to the origin of a person: whether a pure-blooded wizard is in front of him, whether a half-breed, a Muggle-born at all, even a half-human. If acquaintance with him is beneficial, Slughorn will support this acquaintance. And vice versa, whatever the origin of a person, if the relationship with him does not bring any "dividends," the professor will pass by as if there is an empty place in front of him.

So, he calls the pure-blooded sorceress Ginny Weasley and the Muggle-born Hermione Granger to his Slug Club; after learning that the half-giant Hagrid can get hold of a rare and expensive acromantula poison, he helps the forester with the funeral of Aragog, but Draco Malfoy (whose father is sitting in Azkaban) barely deserves a conversation. No wonder he reminds Harry of an old fat spider sitting in the middle of his web and pulling the strings. Slughorn really has the habits of a gray cardinal. Only the goals of this "cardinal" are smaller and... more human or something. A life of comfort is Horace Slughorn's goal, which, in turn, saved Dumbledore's life and almost cost Ron Weasley his life. The fact is that Slughorn received a bottle of excellent oak-matured mead, which he intended to give Dumbledore for Christmas, but he could not part with such a yummy. The bottle stood until March 1, when there was an occasion to drink it with Harry Potter and his friend Ron. But the drink was poisoned. True, Ron, who managed to drink it, was saved by Harry, who found bezoar in the Professor's bag in time. Slughorn later tested all of his supply of drinks on a house elf, which would surely infuriate Hermione.

Horace likes to correspond with his famous former students, which probably flatters his ego.

The final touch to Horace's characterization is his participation in the Battle for Hogwarts. After all, almost all Slytherins refused to defend the castle. However, Slughorn chooses the side of Harry Potter and not the side of Voldemort. And even later, he enters into a battle with the Dark Lord himself, along with Minerva McGonagall and Kingsley Shacklebolt.

Magic abilities

Horace is a pretty smart and well-read wizard. He knows a lot even about really rare and dark magic, but his interest in it is still more theoretical.

Behind the scenes

The role of Horace Slughorn in the films was played by Jim Broadbent.

Interestingly, Broadbent plays the former teacher Severus Snape. However, in real life, the performer of the role of Snape, Alan Rickman, is three years older than his "teacher."

In the film adaptation of the sixth book, Harry finds Slughorn stealing the sprouts of an expensive plant from the school greenhouse. In the book, Professor Sprout herself gives the professor plants for classes. Also, in the film, Slughorn asks Hagrid out loud for permission to remove poison from Aragog, while he does it secretly in the book.

Argus Filch

Argus Filch is an old squib who has been working at Hogwarts as a caretaker since about 1973, replacing Apollyon Pringle in this position.

Filch knows perfectly well all the nooks and crannies in the castle and meticulously keeps order. He loves his cat Mrs. Norris, and there seems to be some kind of mystical connection between them: as soon as the cat sees any disorder, Filch appears almost immediately in this place. Also, some students believe that he is not indifferent to Irma Pince.

Filch tried to master magic with the help of the Kwikspell course but did not succeed at all, which did not add softness and kindness to his bad character. He believes that the order in the school can be restored by resorting to strict disciplinary measures. Therefore, he tirelessly asked Dumbledore to allow flogging and hanging students by their thumbs again. He never got permission from Dumbledore, but Dolores Umbridge gave him such permission almost as soon as she became the headmaster of Hogwarts. The Ambridge fiasco did not teach Filch anything, and after her resignation, the caretaker did not tire of repeating that "Umbridge is the best thing that happened to Hogwarts."

Filch's main enemy is the poltergeist Peeves. This spirit of destruction has caused the poor caretaker so much trouble (and Peeves is a master at these things!). Filch constantly turned to anyone he can with a request to expel the poltergeist from the castle for 25 years of his work. But, according to Rowling, it is impossible to expel Peeves from Hogwarts at all — he is an integral part of the castle.

It is not quite clear what Filch's duties are when more than a hundred elves are engaged in washing, cleaning, cooking in the castle. Fred and George Weasley once mentioned that when Filch ran out of cleaning products, he found a decent supply of them in the Room of Requirement. From which we draw two conclusions: Filch is still cleaning something in the castle, and the magic of the Room of Requirement extends to the squibs.

Interesting facts

1. Filch is more loyal to the students of the Slytherin faculty; at least, he actively supports this faculty at the Gryffindor-Slytherin game in the first film and after the second Slytherin goal, he even actively expresses his joy.

2. According to the film "Harry Potter and the Deathly Hallows: Part 2" (nothing is said in the book on this subject), Filch takes an active part in the defense of Hogwarts and even gets wounded, but immediately after the end of the battle, he starts cleaning the territory.

6. MAJOR MEMBERS OF THE ORDER OF THE PHOENIX

James Potter

James Potter is a pure-blooded wizard, the husband of Lily Potter and the father of Harry Potter. He studied at Hogwarts at the Gryffindor faculty, a member of the first composition of the Order of the Phoenix. He lived a fairly short life.

James comes from a pure-blooded magical family, but the family treated Muggle-born wizards and half-bloods well. James' family was quite well-off.

Fleamont and Euphemia Potter could not have children for a long time. They were already completely desperate when Mrs. Potter, to her surprise, discovered that she was pregnant. James' parents were already in adulthood when he was born. As the only late and desirable child in the family, he grew up surrounded by love and care.

About James' parents, his friend, Sirius Black, says: "I was always a welcome guest at the table of Mr. and Mrs. Potter."

Appearance

James is a thin, brown-eyed young man with tousled black hair. His son is very similar to him. In fact, Harry is a copy of his father, except for his eyes (Harry's mother's eyes are emerald-colored).

Character traits

Most friends and acquaintances talk about James as a cheerful, sociable, talented guy. But the biased Severus Snape considers him a "poseur" and an "upstart." Also, Lily, in her younger years, is annoyed by some of his antics. The truth, as always, lies somewhere in the middle: of course, James had some shortcomings in his childhood and youth — arrogance, a desire to draw attention to himself, but this does not prevent him from being a decent, honest person.

Magical abilities

James Potter was a gifted wizard. He managed to become an animagus (turns into a deer), learned how to summon a Patronus, took part in the development of an interesting magical artifact — a Marauder Map. But this is an incredibly difficult section of magic for a young wizard!

James was a great Quidditch player.

Lily Potter

Lily Potter (née Evans) is a Muggle-born sorceress, the wife of James Potter, the mother of Harry Potter, the sister of Petunia Dursley. She studied at the Gryffindor faculty at Hogwarts, a member of the first composition of the Order of the Phoenix.

Her willingness to die for her son gave Harry Potter protection from the dark magician Voldemort. As a result, the boy became the first person to survive the effects of the killing curse.

Lily Evans was born on January 30, 1960, in the Muggle family of Mr. and Mrs. Evans. She had an older sister, Petunia. The family lived near Spinner's End in the town of Cokeworth. Magic in Lily woke up quite early, and since childhood, she quite consciously knew how to control it. At first, her parents were afraid of her unusual abilities and asked her daughter not to use them, but after her admission to Hogwarts, they were proud that a sorceress was born in their family. Unlike her parents, her older sister Petunia was jealous of Lily's abilities and, therefore, always hated wizards.

Next door to Lily lived a boy, Severus Snape. He had noticed Lily's abilities for a long time, watched her with admiration, and eventually told her about the world of magicians. At first, she was offended when the boy called her a witch, but then the children became friends. Snape told Lily about Hogwarts. Lily was a little afraid of the future life among wizards. Petunia, who does not have magical abilities, was afraid of the magical world in general, but at the same time, she was very jealous of Lily. She also wanted to study at Hogwarts and even wrote a letter to Dumbledore. But he firmly said that this was impossible. In addition, it turned out that Lily and Severus read Dumbledore's answer, which greatly hurt Petunia's feelings. Since Lily's departure to Hogwarts, the relationship between the sisters deteriorated once and for all. After that, they exchanged useless gifts on holidays, but the childhood friendship never returned.

Appearance

Lily is described as a beautiful woman with thick, dark red hair and almond-shaped bright green eyes, inherited by her son and one of her grandchildren.

Personality

Lily was known as an exceptionally kind and talented sorceress who became the Head Girl of the school in her last year at Hogwarts. She was also a favorite student of Professor Horace Slughorn, who noted that she was cheerful and had a talent for potions. He also claimed that such a girl simply could not have enemies, as it was impossible to know Lily and not love her. Remus Lupine noted Lily's ability to discern something good in every person, even if he himself does not see it. At the same time, she was quite a firm person in her beliefs: when Slughorn said that it would be better for her to study in Slytherin, Lily responded in a sharp form with indignation (as Harry himself later answered Sorting Hat); also, she had the strength to break off her relationship with a childhood friend when she realized that he had finally joined the Death Eaters.

Lily, like her husband, was brave and selfless, dying to protect her son. Dumbledore claimed that Harry Potter inherited these qualities from her. It could be stated that Harry got his character from Lily rather than from James, which means that she was a modest, calm, cold-blooded in difficult situations, an honest and fair girl.

Sirius Black

Sirius Black. James Potter's best friend and one of the Marauders, Harry Potter's godfather, a member of the Order of the Phoenix.

He was unfairly accused of the murder of 12 Muggles, which was committed by Peter Pettigrew and was placed in Azkaban prison. After 12 years of imprisonment, he managed to escape.

Family

Born on November 3, 1959. His parents — Orion Black and Walburga Black - were obsessed with the purity of blood. The name Sirius was very common in the Black family, which is probably why the parents gave the newborn such a name. In addition, Sirius had a younger brother-Regulus Black, who completely shared the views of his parents. Orion and Walburga loved both their sons. But Sirius, first out of spite, and then out of his own conviction, becomes in opposition to all pureblood relatives. Kreacher's claim that Sirius "broke his mother's heart" is not without foundation. When entering Hogwarts, young Black gets, and not by chance, into Gryffindor: he did not distinguish between pure-blooded wizards and half-bloods, he considered it beneath his dignity to wander and adapt, build intrigues and pursue a career.

The parents welcomed the decision of Bellatrix and Narcissa to unite with the pureblood Lestrange and Malfoy families, while the name Andromeda Tonks was removed from the tapestry of the Black family tree for marrying a Muggle-born. The same fate befell Uncle Alphard for helping an adult Sirius with money and a house. However, the parents were very pleased with Regulus: he showed all the qualities of "true Blacks" and even became a Death Eater at a very young age. That is, he took the side of Voldemort, whose struggle for granting full power exclusively to pure-blooded wizards was considered a right thing by the older generation of this family.

Studying at Hogwarts

Sirius was the best friend of Harry Potter's father, James Potter since Hogwarts. Besides James, Sirius was friends with Remus Lupine and Peter Pettigrew. The four friends called themselves "Marauders" and often hooligans, sometimes very glared. They made a "Marauder's Map." Shortly after meeting, Sirius and his friends learn that Lupine is a werewolf. But instead of turning their backs on Lupine, the friends decide to become Animagus in order to keep Lupine's company during his nocturnal walks. And by the 5th year, the whole company began to turn into animals without any problems: Sirius - into a big black dog, James - into a big deer, and Peter became a little rat.

Remus Lupin

Remus John Lupin - werewolf, member of the Order of the Phoenix, husband of Nymphadora, father of Teddy Lupin, professor of Defense Against the Dark Arts at Hogwarts in the 1993-1994 academic year, holder of the Order of Merlin I degree (posthumously).

Characteristic

Remus is distinguished by the utmost decency and honesty; he is not capable of lying, even for good purposes. He would rather not say something or say it in other words but not lie. And even then, he will be silent about very little. It's his honesty that Harry likes the most about him.

Unlike previous Defense against the Dark Art professors, Lupine knows his subject very well. In addition, he is an excellent teacher who has a subtle sense of the psychology of those around him, not only children but also adults, who, by the way, are sometimes no better than children. Maybe that's why he, the only one of all the Marauders, was able to establish at least some kind of relationship with Severus Snape.

Remus is objective. He never puts any emotions above facts and above the arguments of reason. For thirteen years, Lupin was sure that Sirius Black had betrayed the Potters, but as soon as he saw Peter Pettigrew alive on Marauder's Map, he rushed to find out the truth and quickly realized who the traitor really was. The same sense of objectivity drives him when he gratefully (!) speaks of Snape as a wonderful potion maker who greatly facilitated his existence.

The safety of the people with whom he communicates is above all for him. That is why he is so afraid of his transformations into a werewolf, that is why Lupin's boggart is a full moon. And that is why his relationship with the woman he loves is developing so unevenly.

But Lupin also has weaknesses. He values the friendship of the Marauders so much that he turns a blind eye to their not always harmless tricks. He understands that this is not good, but he can't help himself. Much later, as a professor at Hogwarts, he hides from Dumbledore that Sirius is able to turn into a dog. He persuades himself that Black gets into the castle by some other, dark method, which does not depend on animagus abilities in any way. After all, if Remus told Dumbledore that three of his students had become unregistered animagus a long time ago, it would mean that even then, during the days of study, the four of them did not justify the teacher's trust, putting their own and other people's lives in danger. Too much would have to be said then. And Lupin was unbearably ashamed just thinking about it.

Comment by J. K. Rowling

Remus Lupin was one of my favorite characters in the whole Harry Potter world. I cried again and again while writing the section of the book about his death.

Lupin's condition-lycanthropy (turning into a werewolf) acted as a metaphor for diseases that are associated with the stigma, such as HIV and AIDS. It is obvious that diseases hiding in the blood are surrounded by a variety of superstitions, perhaps because of taboos that are associated with the blood itself. Wizards are subject to hysteria and prejudice, just like Muggles, and the image of Lupin gave me the opportunity to explore this attitude.

The books never mention the Patronus of Remus Lupin, despite the fact that it was he who taught Harry the complex and unusual art of summoning this entity. This is, in fact, a wolf — an ordinary wolf, not a werewolf. Wolves are family-oriented and not aggressive, but Remus did not like the shape of his Patronus, which was a constant reminder of his illness. He was disgusted by everything wolfish, and often, he deliberately summoned a disembodied patronus, especially if others were watching him.

Arthur Weasley

Arthur Weasley is an employee of the Ministry of Magic, head of the Misuse of Muggle Artefacts Office, later - Office for the Detection and Confiscation of Counterfeit Defensive Spells and Protective Objects. He is the husband of Molly Weasley and the father of their seven children. Member of the second Order of the Phoenix.

He loves Muggles, their inventions and admires their ability to do without magic. He is fond of electrical appliances. On not quite legal grounds, he kept a flying Ford Anglia 105E Deluxe at home — until his youngest son Ron and Harry Potter, having missed the Hogwarts Express, flew it to Hogwarts. As the flying Ford was noticed by many Muggles, both the guys and Arthur himself were punished, and the car that was injured when landing from Whomping Willow escaped to Forbidden Forest.

Appearance

In the books, Arthur Weasley is described as a thin man with a large receding hairline, a tall man with glasses.

In the films, his image is somewhat different: he is of a dense build, with thick hair and normal vision.

It is noteworthy that in the second film, Arthur appears in a very old mantle, which, in general, clearly showed the financial situation of the family, but since the third film, his clothes have improved significantly, and in the sixth film, he already walks around in a new, well-sewn mantle.

Characteristic

Arthur Weasley is not ambitious. For him, a job done in good faith means much more than career growth. He will never stoop to sycophancy. He loves his job and does not need a promotion. He feels good in his place. And that's what his third son, Percy Weasley, blames him for. At the beginning of the fifth book, George, Fred, Ron and Ginny tell Harry about Percy's quarrel with his parents. Among other things, there was an accusation that "because of Dad's filthy reputation (meaning the reputation of a trouble-free, not ambitious worker), we have always been... in general, we didn't have a lot of money."

He is very restrained and non-conflicting. Throughout the six books, only two cases are mentioned when Arthur Weasley lost his temper: This is the quarrel with Percy mentioned above and the case when, as a child, Fred wanted to make an Unbreakable Vow with Ron (an oath, the violation of which entails the death of the violator). The fight described in the second book by Arthur Weasley with Lucius Malfoy, who insulted the Muggles, the parents of Hermione Granger, looks like an easy warm-up in comparison with this.

Behind the scenes

The author of a series of books by J. Rowling admitted that at first, she thought of "killing" Arthur in the Battle for Hogwarts. But then she chose Lupin for this.

Originally, Arthur was supposed to die in the fifth book from a Nagini snake bite, but Rowling changed her mind because if this had happened, the last two books would have been completely different. By turning Ron into a likeness of Harry, into a person who has experienced the loss of his parents, Rowling would have deprived Potter of the refuge that the Weasley family had become for him.

Molly Weasley

Molly Weasley (nee Prewett) is the wife of Arthur Weasley and the mother of their seven children. She is most likely the niece of Ignatius Prewett (who is married to Lucretia Black). A member of the second composition of the Order of the Phoenix.

At Hogwarts, she studied at Gryffindor together with her future husband. She got married early, against the will of her parents, having run away from home.

Characteristic

Despite her kindness, she is quite a domineering woman in everyday life. In fact, she is the true head of the family. At least, it is Molly who runs a rather large family household, she obviously manages finances, solves organizational problems and is mainly engaged in raising children.

Very hardworking. In the entire series of novels, there has never been a case that Molly Weasley did not have breakfast ready in the morning, at whatever hour the characters did not show up in the kitchen. And Ron's mother cooks really tasty, diverse and abundant. She is constantly busy with some household chores, and at Christmas, every member of the family (and Harry, too, since Molly considers him her adopted son) receives a "branded Weasley sweater" tied by the hands of the hostess. At the same time, Mrs. Weasley is not as fixated on cleanliness as Petunia Dursley. If her house has mismatched furniture and the walls do not shine with cleanliness, Molly will not pay attention to it. The microclimate in the family is much more important for her. Even her famous "scolding" is always to the point and without insults.

Magical abilities

Molly masterfully owns a set of housekeeping spells. With the help of such charms, Molly is able to arrange a magnificent feast and clean up the house in just half an hour. Molly also easily knows how to heal minor abrasions, cuts and bruises. It is understandable, in a family with a bunch of mischievous young wizards, that apparently, something happens all the time.

The fact that Molly is a housewife and resorts to magic mainly for all sorts of household chores does not mean at all that she does not own something more powerful. It was the enraged Mrs. Weasley who gave Bellatrix Lestrange such a thrashing that the floor of the Great Hall of Hogwarts under the feet of the sorceresses became hot and cracked and involuntary spectators of the duel huddled against the walls, afraid of falling under a stray spell. And it was Mrs. Weasley who defeated Bellatrix, which three of the last sorceresses — Ginny, Luna and Hermione, had not managed to do at the same time.

Appearance

In the books, Molly is described as a plump, short, red-haired woman. Only once is it mentioned that the color of her eyes is the same as her daughter's (i.e., brown).

Behind the scenes

For Molly, the costumier selected handmade items made in a rustic style or in a style reminiscent of the hippie style of the 60s of the twentieth century.

Alastor Moody

Alastor "Mad-Eye" Moody is a Scottish wizard, an experienced retired Auror.

Alastor is one of the most famous Aurors who fought against the Death Eaters, a kind of legend of the Major Investigation Department: half of the prisoners of Azkaban were caught by him personally. Moody takes an active part in the activities of the Order of the Phoenix.

He owns a magic chest on which the spell Capacious extremis is cast; the chest consists of seven compartments. In the last of them is a kind of dungeon 10 feet deep, where apparently, Moody kept the captured Death Eaters in it.

Appearance and character

As a result of numerous battles with criminals, Moody lost his leg and eye, and his face and hands were disfigured with scars. Moody's prosthetic leg is a wooden clawed paw (in books - right, in films - left). His magical eye, which he uses instead of the lost one, is able to see behind him through walls, objects and doors, as well as through the invisibility cloak. Moody's description features gray hair and a croaking voice.

He has a rude disposition. Moody is cautious and prudent, advises his comrades to be more attentive. He drinks only from his flask and eats his own cooked food. Because of the magic eye and suspicion bordering on paranoia, he received the nickname Mad-Eye.

The constant danger of death has taught Auror to be always on the alert and count on the most unfavorable outcome of events. He kept these habits even in peacetime, which gradually began to cause ridicule from others. Only those who remembered Mad-Eye in the turbulent days retained sincere respect for him. Even his favorite student, the young Auror Nymphadora Tonks, allowed herself to make remarks to Moody when he was completely carried away with his mania for security.

Skills

He's a highly qualified Auror, an outstanding duelist, demonstrating enviable abilities in the field of nonverbal magic. Being an Auror, he must be well-versed not only in defense against the Dark Arts but also in transfiguration, potions and herbology. With equal success, he uses both a magic wand and a staff, which he relies on when walking.

Nymphadora Tonks

Nymphadora Lupine (nee Tonks) - an employee of the Ministry of Magic, Auror, a member of the second composition of the Order of the Phoenix, has the abilities of a metamorph. This means that she can magically change her appearance with ease without resorting to spells or potions.

Nymphadora often appears in public with pink hair, which, apparently, most corresponds to her mischievous character.

Personality

Tonks has an easy character and treats everything with humor. This is a brave girl, always ready to help. However, she has one drawback that forces others to take this help very carefully: Tonks is terribly clumsy. Also, she hates being called by her full name and just prefers Tonks.

Despite her youth, Tonks is not afraid to express her opinion and object to Mad-Eye. Sometimes, she even teases the legendary Auror!

Appearance

Tonks-metamorphmagus most often took the form of a young sorceress with a pale, pointed face in the shape of a heart and short, sticking-out-in-all-directions hair the color of bright pink gum. Probably, the real color of her hair is mouse-like because this is exactly what her hair was during the depression when she could not control her abilities.

During the operations of the Order, the Nymphadora took the form of an old lady with tightly curled gray curls.

Q. What Kind Of Cereal Do They Serve At Hogwarts?
A. Hufflepuffs

JOKES HP

7. VOLDEMORT AND HIS MAIN FOLLOWERS

Tom Riddle

Tom Marvolo Riddle is the main antagonist in the Harry Potter series of novels; a dark wizard who has great magical power and has almost achieved immortality with the help of black magic or rather, with the help of Horcruxes. In the wizarding world, he is better known as Lord Voldemort.

They are afraid of him to such an extent that even his name, as a rule, is not pronounced. Most heroes call him You-Know-Who or He-Who-Must-Not-Be-Named, and his followers, the Death Eaters, call him The Dark Lord.

Harry Potter, however, was not afraid to say his name initially because he grew up among Muggles and first heard about Voldemort only at the age of eleven. He did not know about his villainies and did not have the prejudices inherent in the majority. Later, in a circle of other wizards, respecting their feelings, he calls the Dark Lord You-Know-Who, but in the end, following Dumbledore's example, he makes it a rule to always call him by his first name. Over time, with some caution, his example is followed by Hermione Granger and Ginny Weasley. Some members of the Order of the Phoenix, such as Sirius Black, Remus Lupin and Albus Dumbledore, always called Voldemort's full name without any hesitation.

Appearance and personal qualities

The reborn Voldemort is described as having very pale skin, a chalk-white and skull-like face, snake-like nostrils, red eyes with vertical pupils, a tall skeletal body and long thin hands with unnaturally long fingers. Earlier, during his studies at Hogwarts, he was described as a very attractive young man with an aristocratic bearing, with thin features, sunken cheeks, dark eyes and black hair. Albus Dumbledore believes that such significant changes in appearance were caused by the actions and deeds of Tom himself: "Over the years, Lord Voldemort increasingly lost his human form, and the transformations that took place with him had only one explanation: the mutilation of his soul went far beyond what ordinary evil is capable of."

Voldemort hates Muggles and Muggle-born wizards. This is all the more surprising when you find out that Voldemort himself is a half-breed. Obviously, resentment at the mother who accepted her death and left her newborn son defenseless in this world, and even greater resentment at the father who abandoned the mother before the birth of the child, played a role in the formation of this relationship. Resentment that his father, with his Muggle origin, "spoiled" such a brilliant pedigree (of course, the Riddle are direct descendants of Salazar Slytherin himself!). Resentment that his mother gave him such an ordinary name, and even in honor of some Muggle father, as if erasing the bright, unique personality of his son. All together prompted Tom Riddle to invent a sonorous name for himself and by all means to prove to those around him and to himself that there were no Muggles among his ancestors and could not have been. At the age of sixteen, Tom Riddle killed his his parents and changed his name, going by an anagram from the name "Tom Marvolo Riddle" to "Lord Voldemort," apparently psychologically renouncing his origin in this way. However, Voldemort does not hide the fact that he is a half-breed, as he publicly talks about his Muggle father.

Voldemort has advanced in the study of magic, especially in the field of the Dark Arts, perhaps more deeply than any living wizard. But in two cases, according to him, he could not remember in time about important things: the healing effect of the tears of the phoenix and the power of ancient magic associated with love and self-sacrifice (things that are beyond his understanding, according to Dumbledore).

Between the fates of Tom Riddle and Harry Potter, you can see a lot in common — both were orphans, grew up among Muggles not in the most successful conditions until they were accepted into Hogwarts, which both began to consider their home. Both characters have black hair, delicate facial features and the ability to talk to snakes. This illustrates one of the ideas of the series, expressed by Dumbledore, that the essence of a person is determined by his choice and not by his abilities.

The author of a series of books about Harry Potter, J. K. Rowling, suggested that Voldemort's main fear is "humiliating death," and his boggart will be his own lifeless body. In the Mirror of Erised, showing the most ardent desire of the beholder, he would see himself as omnipotent and immortal.

If we talk about personal qualities, Voldemort can be called a cautious, quick-witted and calm strategist. In the fourth and fifth years of Harry Potter's studies at Hogwarts, Voldemort planned long, year-long operations: the first was connected with his return to the body, the second with the invasion of the Department of Mysteries.

Voldemort, so afraid of his own death, is absolutely indifferent to someone else's. He kills with amazing ease, especially if the person can no longer be useful to him. This lack of basic empathy for anyone is shocking, even to his followers.

Bellatrix Lestrange

Bellatrix Lestrange (née Black) is a pure-blooded sorceress, a Death Eater, the most zealous henchwoman of Voldemort. A professional in combat magic: inferior in skill except to the Dark Lord himself. She is prone to madness,is very cruel and insidious, a great tactician and strategist.

Bellatrix comes from an ancient magical family of Blacks, whose representatives were obsessed with the purity of blood. She is the eldest daughter of Cygnus Black and Druella Rosier and has two sisters, Andromeda Tonks and Narcissa Malfoy, as well as two cousins, Sirius and Regulus Black.

Bellatrix studied at Hogwarts at the faculty of Slytherin under Horace Slughorn at the same time as Lucius Malfoy, Avery, Weasley and many other heroes of the book. But Bellatrix's younger sister Narcissa married Lucius, and she herself married one of Voldemort's school friends, Rodolphus Lestrange. Although, as it turns out in the seventh book, the only one she loved all her life was the Dark Lord.

Appearance

Bellatrix is described as a tall woman with "heavy eyelids" and a crown of shiny black hair, whose face looks withered and like a skull after a long imprisonment in Azkaban, and her hair is long and unkempt. Although the dark sorceress has retained the remnants of her former beauty, fourteen years spent in captivity have greatly affected her appearance. But one thing remains unchanged even years later- her arrogance and fanatical devotion to his Dark Lord.

Personality and character traits

By nature, Bellatrix Lestrange is very hot-tempered, somewhat hysterical and emotional, which is constantly emphasized as a difference from her sister Narcissa. During the Battle of the Department of Mysteries, Lucius Malfoy has to pull Bella up several times so that she does not lose her temper and derail the operation. It's hard to say if she's always been like this or if the years with the dementors have not passed without a trace. The Death Eater herself, according to Snape, has many memories of how bad it was in Azkaban.

Another characteristic feature of Madame Lestrange is bloodthirstiness and an undisguised tendency to sadism. She is always ready to use the Cruciatus and torture her victim for as long as she wants. Torture with a feverish, crazy fanatical gleam in her eyes became her "calling card." She is aggressive and prefers to solve all problems with the help of force. She has no feeling of pity at all. Often, Bellatrix is guided solely by the wishes of the Dark Lord and the desire to please him. The only people to whom she is more or less soft (not counting "her Dark Lord," of course) are her sister Cissy and her nephew Draco. It is noticeable that family ties mean a lot to her if relatives do not belong to the category of "blood traitors" (as Nymphadora Tonks and Sirius Black had the misfortune to be convinced of).

Magic skills and abilities

Bellatrix Lestrange is an excellent duelist, who perfectly owns combat magic.

Lucius Malfoy

Lucius Malfoy II; April 4, 1954, death eater, husband of Narcissa Malfoy, father of Draco Malfoy and grandfather of Scorpius Malfoy. Lucius Malfoy studied at the Slytherin faculty, and in his last year, was the head boy of the school. Lucius had always been proud of his pureblood ancestry and despised Muggle-born wizards.

Lucius Malfoy was born into a very ancient, wealthy and noble pureblood family. He grew up in luxury in the family estate, a magnificent mansion in Wiltshire. Since childhood, Lucius has been taught that he is special because: firstly, he is a wizard; secondly, he is pure-blooded, and thirdly, he is a Malfoy, whose family inspires confidence in the eyes of the magical community and has great influence in the Ministry of Magic. Lucius' father, Abraxas Malfoy, taught him to maintain above all prudence and respectable appearance, demonstrating a privileged position among their kind, as well as to show respect to representatives of the ruling class, from whom the family can benefit enormously. In addition, since the Malfoys are supporters of the superiority of pure blood, Lucius was proud of his origin from an early age and communicated with children exclusively from proven pureblood families.

Personal qualities

Ironic, self-confident, ambitious, he always goes to the intended goal without noticing obstacles. Artistic, quirky, cautious, he is cold and contemptuous of everyone whom he considers inferior in social status. He is characterized by flexibility of mind and behavior, easily maneuvers in any circumstances ("Lucius, my slippery friend..."). Outwardly accepting any image convenient for oneself, internally, it always preserves its I.

Interesting facts

In the film adaptation of "Harry Potter and the Order of the Phoenix", the prophecy in the Department of Mysteries is accidentally shattered by Lucius Malfoy; however, in the book, it was done by Neville Longbottom.

In the film adaptations of the last book, Lucius completely neglected himself (he didn't even shave). Apparently, Malfoy was so influenced by stress, firstly, from a whole year of imprisonment, and secondly, from the fact that Lucius made many mistakes that the Dark Lord was not used to forgiving.

Peter Pettigrew

Peter Pettigrew, nicknamed Wormtail, is the fourth creator of Marauder's Map, one of the former school friends of James Potter, Sirius Black and Remus Lupin. A former Gryffindor, a servant of Voldemort.

An unregistered animagus, capable of turning into a rat, was awarded the Order of Merlin First Class (posthumously) in 1981.

Peter Pettigrew is a weak man and needs a patron. During his school years at Hogwarts, James Potter, Harry's father, acted as a patron.

Betrayal

Shortly after James Potter and Lily Evans had a son, Harry, they learned that Lord Voldemort wanted to kill him. Friends decided to apply the spell of Fidelius to the young Potter family. This is a disguising spell that reliably hides someone who wants to hide. No one, except the Keeper of the Secret, can find the hidden one, "even if he sticks his nose in the window of their house." The Potters wanted to make Black the keeper, but at the very last moment, Sirius persuaded them to appoint Pettigrew as the Keeper. Shortly before that, it became known that one of the Potter friends had defected to Voldemort's side, and Black suspected Lupin of treachery. Sirius decided that no one would think that Peter had been appointed as the guardian.

Only Sirius, Peter and, of course, James and Lily knew that the Keeper of the Potter secret was not Black but Pettigrew. The calculation was that the Death Eaters would hunt for Black: even if they could not get the secret out of him, the spell would weaken with the death of the Keeper. And this "deception" would allow the true Keeper of Pettigrew to remain in the shadows at all, which meant that the Potters could also hope that they would be relatively safe for a while. But everything turned out differently. Peter Pettigrew always needed a powerful patron, and when Lord Voldemort gained strength, the Wormtail went over to him. And as an "entrance fee," he gave him the location of the Potter family.

After the murder of James and Lily, Sirius Black, of course, realized who the traitor was. He caught up with Pettigrew in the middle of a street full of Muggles, but Wormtail shouted to the whole street that Black was a traitor and then faked his death: he set off an explosion in the middle of the street, killing twelve Muggles, and left his severed finger at the explosion site as proof of his death. Sirius Black was charged with the murder of Muggles and Peter Pettigrew and sentenced to life imprisonment in Azkaban.

Personality

At school, Peter did not shine with either knowledge or ingenuity, but he could always count on the help of other Marauders. He paid them with enthusiastic reviews (at any age, it is flattering when your achievements are noticed and appreciated) and a willingness to support any trick. At the same time, Pettigrew prudently swallowed all voluntary or involuntary insults. He was particularly hurt by Sirius, who could offend in passing with a word worse than someone else with an action. At the same time, friend James rarely reproached Black for this, and Remus, if he stood up for Peter, did it extremely rarely and in a very streamlined form. It is likely that Peter, outwardly not giving himself away, was accumulating these grievances...

8. MAJOR EMPLOYEES OF THE MINISTRY OF MAGIC

Cornelius Fudge

Cornelius Oswald Fudge is a wizard. In 1981, he was the deputy head of the Department of Emergency Situations. From 1990 to 1996 — British Minister for Magic. Since mid-July 1996, he became a consultant for relations with the British Prime Minister of Muggles. Fudge is first mentioned in the first book, "Harry Potter and the Philosopher's Stone," and appears in the book "Harry Potter and the Chamber of Secrets."

He is a knight of the Order of Merlin of the first degree, the highest award among magicians. Fudge awarded the Order to himself for his phenomenal career, but this caused a lot of controversy in society.

Magic power and skills

Fudge is pretty good at Transfiguration and non-verbal spells. During visits to the Muggle prime minister, he effortlessly transforms a teacup into a jerboa and creates whiskey glasses out of thin air without speaking.

In addition, the highest NEWT scores are required for admission to the Ministry, so it can be argued with a certain degree of probability that Fudge also owns other magical disciplines.

Assumptions

Based on the description of the appearance and politics of Fudge, it can be assumed that his prototype was British Prime Minister Neville Chamberlain, notorious for his policy of "appeasement." In an attempt to avoid a world war, he preferred to ignore the danger of Nazi Germany and trying to "satisfy their hunger" with new lands and turning a blind eye to their militarization, in fact, only made the situation worse.

Behind the scenes

Cornelius Fudge was played by British actor Robert Hardy in the films.

The news of Cornelius ' resignation is announced in the sixth book, while in the film series, in the fifth.

In addition, in the film adaptation of Harry Potter and the Order of the Phoenix, Fudge is not shown to be more antagonistic to Harry and Dumbledore than in the book. Perhaps this was simply because he was not given a lot of screen time or because the rivalry between some of the characters is less demonstrated in the movies than in the novels.

The books always mention that Fudge wears a green bowler hat. In the film, he wears black all the time.

Rufus Scrimgeour

Rufus Scrimgeour is the Minister of Magic of Great Britain, the successor of Cornelius Fudge. First mentioned as the head of the Auror Office. With the outbreak of the Second Magical War, he succeeded Cornelius Fudge as Minister of Magic. He is brave, smart, prudent and self-contained. However, he is no stranger to careerism and a thirst for power, although he is more cautious about these goals than Fudge. Scrimgeour's policy was distinguished by more consistent and decisive steps in the fight against Lord Voldemort and his Death Eaters. True, Scrimgeour could not avoid the typical mistake of his predecessor. Afraid to publicly admit the power of Voldemort, Scrimgeour is not looking for allies in the fight against the Dark Lord. The Ministry covers up the lack of real victories over the enemy with boastful reports, arresting not real Death Eaters but the first people who have aroused suspicion in any way.

By continuing the policy of silencing problems and creating only the appearance of the well-being and safety of the magical community, Scrimgeour thereby made the Ministry of Magic an easy prey for Death Eaters. The latter used officials under their control, who successfully carried out a coup in the Ministry and gave it to the Dark Lord's people...

Dolores Umbridge

Dolores Jane Umbridge - Assistant to the Minister for Magic Cornelius Fudge and the next two ministers. In fact, she acts like a chain dog, being loyal to the current minister, regardless of how much his policy differs from the policy of the previous one. At the peak of her ambitions, she volunteered to teach Defense against the Dark Arts at Hogwarts, later became the Hogwarts High Inquisitor, the director, and after failing at this job, returned to the Ministry. She showed particularly vigorous activity in the year of Voldemort's reign as the head of the Muggle-Born Registration Commission. For crimes against Muggle-borns, she was subsequently sentenced to life imprisonment in Azkaban.

Early years

Dolores was the eldest child and the only daughter in the family of wizard Orford Umbridge and Muggle Ellen Cracknell, who also had a son Squib. Dolores' parents were not happily married, and she secretly despised them both: Orford - for lack of ambition (he worked in the Magical Maintenance Department at the Ministry of Magic and never got promoted), and Ellen - for capriciousness, untidiness and Muggle pedigree. The father and daughter blamed Ellen for the lack of magical abilities of Dolores' brother. As a result, when Dolores was 15 years old, her family broke up: Ellen and her son went back to the Muggle world, leaving Dolores with her father. Dolores never saw her mother and brother again, never started a conversation about any of them, and from now on, pretended to everyone she met that she was a pure-blooded sorceress.

Appearance and character

Dolores Umbridge is a squat, rather fat and plump woman, resembling a large pale toad in her appearance. Even her favorite little black velvet bow on her head resembles a fat fly that the "toad" is about to eat. She has a broad, loose face and a short neck, her eyes are large, round and slightly protruding, with leathery bags, and her mouth is wide and flabby with very sharp teeth. Dolores's hair is half-gray, mouse-brown, curly and short-cropped. Umbridge has a thin, girlish, unstable voice with a breathy sound that sounds venomous and flattering, and her silvery laugh makes Harry's hair stand on end. And her soft "cough, cough" became a trademark. Dolores has thick stubby fingers, on which she prefers to wear old-fashioned ugly rings.

Umbridge chooses clothes in various shades of pink. Harry notices that she looks "like someone's eternally unmarried aunt." Probably, Dolores has absolutely trouble with taste: she can put on a fluffy knitted blouse over her mantle and tie a bright pink ribbon to match it on her head or a mantle with a bright floral pattern, like a tablecloth on the table. She also often walks around with a tasteless colorful bag, and, of course, almost all of her things, right down to stationery, are pink.

She likes to control literally every little thing, and anyone who undermines her authority or whose worldview differs from hers should be punished immediately. She enjoys the process of subjugating and humiliating others. Umbridge doesn't have much magical power, she has big character problems. She is quite gullible (otherwise, how could Hermione have fooled her so easily?), and in the same episode in the film, she utters a strange phrase: "(scared) You tricked me, didn't you? Is he not here? (plaintively, almost sobbing) You know... I hate children..." It is worth noting separately that if Umbridge had not been conceived as a supporting antagonist, then perhaps she could have helped the main characters. But she fully supports the policy of her leadership and behaves like the main character of A.P. Chekhov's story "Chameleon."

Behind the scenes

Professor Umbridge is the least attractive character in the entire series. J.K. Rowling noted that

Umbridge was "an unpleasant part of the job."

The only employee who sincerely supported Dolores was Argus Filch. For him, Dolores was the best thing that happened at Hogwarts. It's even possible that Filch had romantic feelings for her...

Author's comment

Once, many years ago, I attended classes where I had to communicate with a teacher whom I disliked at first sight.

This woman has responded a hundredfold to my dislike. I cannot explain why she and I were imbued with such a sudden, sincere and (at least on my part) unaccountable hatred for each other. The first thing that comes to mind when I think of her is her love for sugary, elegant accessories. I especially remember her tiny plastic hairpin, a pale lemon-colored bow, which she wore on her short curly hair. My eyes kept bumping into this little hairpin that would have been more appropriate for a three-year-old girl. She was a rather stocky woman of not the first youth, and her tendency to wear frills where they simply should not have been and to carry small handbags that she seemed to have borrowed from a child's locker, in my opinion, was out of harmony with her character, which I would have found not at all soft, innocent and simple-minded.

I am always careful to talk about such sources of inspiration because it infuriates me when my words are interpreted incorrectly. This woman WAS NOT "that same Dolores Umbridge." She didn't look like a toad, she didn't have sadistic tendencies, she wasn't cruel to me or anyone else. And I've never heard her make statements similar to Umbridge's (in fact, I've never known her well enough to know enough about her views and preferences, which makes my dislike of her even less justified). However, to tell the truth, I borrowed from her and then greatly exaggerated the passion for the cloying way of dressing, and that's why I remembered that very tiny pale lemon plastic bow when I placed a fly-like ornament on Dolores Umbridge's head.

Dolores, who is one of the characters to whom I have a clear antipathy, has mixed features borrowed from such memories described above and from various other sources. Her desire to control, punish and inflict pain in the name of law and order, I think, should be condemned in the same way as Voldemort's unadorned pursuit of evil.

TOP 7 POTIONS IN HARRY POTTER

The students at Hogwarts learn more of their magical skills by advancing in a variety of areas, for instance, learning dueling techniques for the Dark Arts Defense, changing themselves and things in the process of Transfiguration, or creating flying prowess by the practice of Quidditch.

Yet an always-underestimated subject is Potions, which is a magical field that teaches wizards and witches to infuse several wonderful mixtures ranging from mystical to deadly. While Professor Snape is nonetheless a harsh teacher to non-Slytherin students, Potions is all time an amazing class that Harry succeeded to get an "Exceeds Expectations" during his O.W.L. examinations, and many potions helped the Selected One in his travels multiple times.

As there are lots of mysterious tonics throughout the Wizarding World, the question is which spirits are to reign supreme?

7. Wolfsbane Potion

Ingredients: Wolfsbane (presumably others as well).

Effect: Relieves the effects of lycanthropy.

Wolfsbane Potion is not to cure; rather, it eases the symptoms of lycanthropy, the disease from which Remus Lupin is suffering. Lycanthropy is basically a modest term used for a werewolf, and while Wolfsbane does not avoid the change under a full moon, it has an ability to transform its user into a regular drowsy wolf rather than a vicious werewolf. Those who consume Wolfsbane are allowed to maintain their memories after the transformation.

The way it is helpful to lycanthropy-inflicted wizards, Wolfsbane is also delicate to craft, and the ingredients are too expensive to find, which means several werewolves have failed to surely ingest it. Remus Lupin agrees to teach Defense Against the Dark Arts during Harry's third year in the Prisoner of Azkaban book. The condition on which Remus agrees is that Severus Snape continuously makes Wolfsbane for his use, a term Dumbledore mindfully agrees to.

6. Skele-Gro

Ingredients: Chinese chomping cabbage, puffer-fish, scarab beetles.

Effect: Makes the lost bones regrow.

This is a vile-tasting and painful potion. Skele-Gro is truly a bold apothecary tool, capable of regenerating the lost bones. Madam Pomfrey helps Harry's right arm to recover in the Chamber of Secrets after Gilderoy Lockhart missteps an attempt to heal Harry after his severe injury in a Quidditch match.

In book seven Deathly Hallows, Fleur Delacour also made use of Skele-Gro to the goblin Griphook to treat the leg injuries he obtained during the raid into Gringotts bank.

5. Invisibility Potion

Ingredients: Cherries (presumably more).

Effect: Renders one temporarily invisible.

This was a convenient alternative to the Invisibility Cloak or Disillusionment charm. The canon of this potion can be questioned because it only expresses itself in chosen Harry Potter video games. However, it gives the same important effect as Harry's notorious cloak, which made a person invisible to the naked eye.

To avoid detection is much easier while one is invisible, which Harry and his friends successively prove. For a moment, imagine the advantage of drinking this liquid before war—the enemy simply can't hit what they can't see with their eyes. Floating like a butterfly, stinging like an invisible bee.

4. Veritaserum

Ingredients: Unknown.

Effect: Forces the user to tell the truth when questioned.

This is considered to be the most powerful truth serum because Veritaserum makes its user answer anything asked to them with accuracy. This provides a convenient tool for the justice system of wizarding, given all the disguises and tricks gained by other potions and spells.

It was said that a corresponding antidote or sufficient Occlumency skill could resist Veritaserum, which mostly made it an ineffective tool in court proceedings. Given all the counter forces in Goblet of Fire, Veritaserum was used by Dumbledore on Barty Crouch Jr. to expose his impression of Alastor "Mad-Eye" Moody. As violent as this secret-revealing mixture is, Crouch could be seen using an even more powerful potion than this to maintain his charade.

3. Polyjuice Potion

Ingredients: Lacewing flies, leeches, knotgrass, fluxweed, and a hair from the desired form

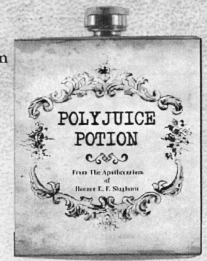

Effect: Changes appearance to match the hair's bearer.

Harry and Ron used this potion in Chamber of Secrets to get information from Draco Malfoy by masquerading as Vincent Crabbe and Gregory Goyle. The Polyjuice Potion completely alters a mystic's appearance and alters the personality to mimic an individual, which is greatly helpful in subterfuge. It is only effective when used with beings of the same species. Hermione, due to stealing the cat hair, morphs accidentally.

Polyjuice Potion provides a challenge for experienced wizards and witches to brew. It also requires a lot of attention and time to settle. In addition to Harry, Ron, and Barty Crouch's uses, Polyjuice was also helpful for Draco's smuggling of Death Eaters into Hogwarts, the gang's infiltration of the Ministry of Magic, and Harry's plan to deceive Delphi in the Cursed Child. Though it is very powerful, Polyjuice users must take precautionary measures as the effect fades after an hour.

2. Felix Felicis

Ingredients: Ashwinder egg, squill bulb, murtlap tentacle.

Effect: Temporarily grants the recipient luck.

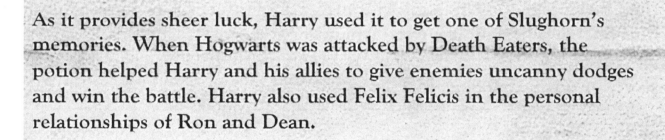

Felix Felicis is very hard to brew as it takes six months and is dangerous when the proportion of fusion is not correct. As it makes an ordinary day into extraordinary, it is banned in official events and exams.

As it provides sheer luck, Harry used it to get one of Slughorn's memories. When Hogwarts was attacked by Death Eaters, the potion helped Harry and his allies to give enemies uncanny dodges and win the battle. Harry also used Felix Felicis in the personal relationships of Ron and Dean.

1. Elixir of Life

Ingredients: The Sorcerer's Stone (or Philosopher's Stone, for non-Americans).

Effect: Extends one's life indefinitely.

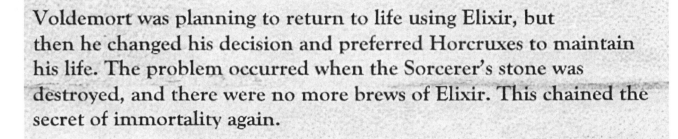

This potion extends life as it is derived from the Sorcerer's stone, and the creator of this stone and his wife lived for 600 years. One can't be sure if it extends life or makes one immortal.

Voldemort was planning to return to life using Elixir, but then he changed his decision and preferred Horcruxes to maintain his life. The problem occurred when the Sorcerer's stone was destroyed, and there were no more brews of Elixir. This chained the secret of immortality again.

LIST OF SPELLS

Need to unlock a door? Fix a broken object? Disarm an enemy? There's a Harry Potter spell for that! In the Harry Potter universe, there is a spell to fulfill any need, from the every day to the extraordinary. Below is a list of Harry Potter spells and what they do.

A

1. Aberto

Classification: Charm

Say: Ah-bare-toh

Interpretation: This word is a spell, which is uttered to open the doors.

2. Accio

Classification: Charm

Interpretation: This word is a spell, which is used to call something towards the caster. The object that is being called can be or cannot be in the view of the caster. The caster should have a clear object in his mind before summoning it.

Spell class: Summoning Charm

Seen/Specified: Harry Potter used this spell to summon his broom in his tournament in 1994. The spell was used to summon Portkey, who helped Voldemort to escape, and it was also used to summon the Death Eaters in the Little Hangleton Graveyard in 1995. When Harry fell during the Battle of Seven Potters, he used this spell to summon Hagrid. Molly Weasley and the Twins used this spell to get the twins candy and to summon the brooms, respectively.

Etymology: From Latin the word accio means "I call".

Say: AK-see-oh

3. Alarte Ascendare

Classification: Charm

Interpretation: This spell is used if the target is in the air and the caster wants to shoot it.

Seen/Specified: In 1992, Gilderoy Lockhart used this spell.

Say: a-LAR-tay a-SEN-der-ay

4. Aguamenti

Classification: Conjuration, Charm

Interpretation: This spell produces ca lean and drinkable water jet.

Spell class: Water-Making Spell

Seen/Specified: In 1994, Fleur Delacour used this spell to extinguish her skirt, which started burning due to the dragon flame while fighting. In 1997, this spell was used by Harry two times in the same night. He used it once to help Dumbledore get a drink and the second time to help douse Hagrid's hut.

Say: AH-gwah-MEN-tee

5. Alohomora

Classification: Charm

Interpretation: Used to open locked doors or other locked objects.

Spell class: Unlocking Charm

Seen/Specified: Hermione Granger used it in 1991 to allow herself and friends to reach the Third-floor corridor at her school, which was not allowed to be accessed. She used this spell again two years later when she wanted to free Sirius's cell in her teacher's prison room.

Say: ah-LOH-ho-MOR-ah

6. Amato Animo Animato Animagus

Classification: Transfiguration

Interpretation: The witches or wizards who can transform into animagus use this spell in the process of their transformation. It is necessary that this spell should be recited at sunrise or sunset, and it should be recited before the consumption of the animagus potion. While placing the wand's tip over one's heart, the chant is recited.

Spell class: Animagus Spell

Say: ah-MAH-toh ah-NEE-moh ah-nee-MAH-toh an-a-MAY-jus

7. Anapneo

Classification: Vanishment, Healing Spell

Interpretation: This chant is a healing spell, which clears the airway of the target by vanishing whatever it is choking on.

Seen/Specified: Horace Slughorn used this spell on Marcus Belby in 1996 when the latter was choking on a pheasant.

Say: ah-NAP-nee-oh

8. Anteoculatia

Classification: Hex

Interpretation: This spell grows antlers on the target.

Seen/Specified: Pansy Parkinson's antlers grew by the use of this spell in 1996.

Say: an-tee-oh-kyoo-LAY-chee-ah

9. Aparecium

Classification: Charm

Interpretation: This spell makes writings visible that are written by invisible ink or any other substance.

Spell class: Revealing Charm

Seen/Specified: Hermione Granger used this spell in 1993 to attempt to reveal hidden writing, which was written in a diary.

Say: AH-par-EE-see-um

10. Appare Vestigium

Classification: Charm

Interpretation: This spell reveals traces, tracks, and footprints of magic.

Spell class: Tracking Spell

Seen/Specified: While searching for Porpentina Goldstein, Newton Scamander used this spell.

Say: ah-PAR-ay ves-TEE-jee-um

11. Arania Exumai

Classification: Charm

Interpretation: This spell is used to drive away spiders, including their bigger species.

Spell class: Spider repelling spell

Seen/Specified: By using this spell, Jacob's sibling repelled an Acromantula, which was guarding the Forest Vault in the Forbidden Forest.

Say: ah-RAHN-ee-a EKS-su-may

12. Arresto Momentum

Classification: Charm

Interpretation: This spell decreases the speed of targets. It also decreases the speed of the caster, if required. Daisy Pennifold invented it in 1711 for use on the Quaffle in Quidditch.

Spell class: Slowing Charm

Seen/Specified: Dumbledore used this spell in 1993 to save one of his students from a fall.

Say: ah-REST-oh mo-MEN-tum

13. Ascendio

Classification: Charm

Interpretation: This spell floats the caster in the air, and it works underwater as well. If chanted underwater, the spell propels the caster towards the surface of the water.

Seen/Specified: Harry Potter used this spell in the Second Task of the Triwizard Tournament in 1995. The spell propelled him towards the surface of the lake.

Say: ah-SEN-dee-oh

14. Avada Kedavra

Classification: Curse

Interpretation:

This spell causes death instantaneously, and there is no counter-spell for it except loving sacrifice. The flash of green light and rushing noises is seen and heard, respectively.

Harry Potter was able to escape death from this spell many times. Once, he escaped due to his mother's sacrifice. The other time, he escaped as the core of his wand and his enemy's wand was the same.

Spell class: Killing Curse

Seen/Specified: Voldemort used it to kill many of his victims without any remorse.

Say: ah-VAH-dah keh-DAV-rah

15. Avenseguim

Classification: Charm

Interpretation: The spell is used to turn any object into a tracking device.

Seen/Specified: In 1927, Newton Scamander used this spell while searching for Porpentina Goldstein. He tracked the origin of a feather, which came from the hat of Yusuf Kama.

Say: ah-ven-SEH-gwim

16. Avis

Classification: Charm, Conjuration

Interpretation: It can conjure a flock of birds from the wand tip of the caster. The spell can be used offensively as well.

Spell class: Bird-Conjuring Charm

Seen/Specified: Mr. Ollivander tested the wand of Viktor Krum with this spell. Hermione Granger used this spell offensively against Ron Weasley.

Say: AH-viss

B

1. Baubillious

Interpretation: This spell causes a bolt of white light and is of a damaging nature. The exact effects of this spell are unknown.

Say: baw-BILL-ee-us

2. Bombarda

Classification: Charm

Interpretation: It causes a small explosion.

Spell class: Exploding Charm

Seen/Specified: When Hermione Granger freed Sirius Black from prison in 1994, this spell was used.

Say: bom-BAR-dah

3. Brackium Emendo

Classification: Healing Spell, Charm

Interpretation: It is claimed that this spell can heal broken bones, but this has never been proved practically.

Seen/Specified: Gilderoy Lockhart used this spell on Harry Potter when his arm was broken by Bludger. It didn't heal his arm and transformed it into rubber.

Say: BRA-key-um ee-MEN-doh

C

1. Cantis

Classification: Jinx

Interpretation: This spell makes victims sing songs uncontrollably.

Seen/Specified: Hogwarts professors used this spell to enchant suits of armour.

Say: CAN-tiss

2. Cave inimicum

Classification: Charm

Interpretation: This spell produces a wall or boundary to keep the caster hidden from the view of others.

Seen/Specified: Hermione Granger used it multiple times in 1997, 1998. This spell protected the tent, which she shared with Harry Potter and Ron Weasley.

Say: CAH-vay uh-NIM-i-kuhm

3. Circumrota

Classification: Charm

Interpretation: This spell rotates the targeted objects.

Seen/Specified: Leta Lestrange used this spell to rotate a record tower in the Records Room at the French Ministry of Magic Headquarters to see Newton Scamander and Porpentina Goldstein, who was hiding behind the tower.

Say: SIR-cum-roh-tuh

4. Cistem Aperio

Classification: Charm

Interpretation: The spell opens boxes and trunks.

Seen/Specified: Tom Riddle used this spell to open the chest to find Aragog hidden in the chest.

Say: SIS-tem uh-PE-ree-o

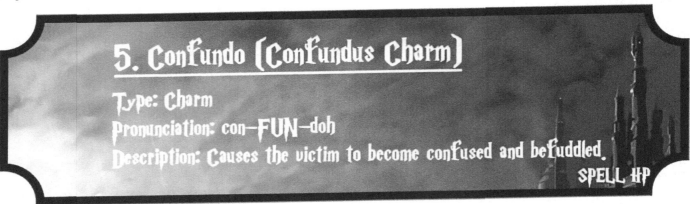

5. Confundo (Confundus Charm)

Type: Charm

Pronunciation: con—FUN—doh

Description: Causes the victim to become confused and befuddled.

SPELL HP

6. Crinus Muto

Classification: Transfiguration

Interpretation: This chant changes the color and style of hair.

Seen/Specified: In 1996, the color of Harry's eyebrows turned yellow. It is considered that this happened due to this spell.

7. Crucio

Classification: Curse

Interpretation: The victim of this curse starts feeling intense pain, and this curse can make the victim crazy. The pain of this curse is equal to hot knives driven inside the body of the target. The caster must be very angry at the victim and should be cursing this out of anger. The caster suffers a life sentence, for this is an unforgivable curse.

Seen/Specified: This curse is used many times after the fourth book.

Say: KROO-see-oh

D

1. Densaugeo

Classification: Hex

Interpretation: This word is a hex and causes rapid growth of teeth of victim. It can also be used to grow the lost teeth of a victim.

Seen/Specified: In 1994, when the spell of Draco Malfoy returned upon Hermione Granger, her teeth were so big that they crossed her collar before she was forced to run to the hospital to get them cut. Harry's teeth were mended by this spell in 1997.

Say: den-SAW-jee-oh

2. Deprimo

Classification: Charm

Interpretation: This charm can blast the holes present on the surface.

Seen/Specified: Hermione Granger used this spell in 1998 to blast a hole through the living room floor of Xenophilius Lovegood's house.

Say: deh-PREEM-oh

3. Depulso

Classification: Charm

Interpretation: This charm is the opposite of summoning charm and sends the target away from the caster.

Spell class: Banishing Charm

Seen/Specified: This charm has been used multiple times in 1993 and 1995.

Say: deh-PUL-soh

4. Descendo

Classification: Charm

Interpretation: This charm sends the target downwards.

Seen/Specified: In 1997, Ron used this charm on the stairs in his bedroom to descend. In the same year, Crabbe used it to cause a wall of rubbish behind which Ron was hiding.

Say: deh-SEN-doh

5. Diffindo

Classification: Charm

Interpretation: This charm is used to cut objects with precision.

Spell class: Severing Charm

Seen/Specified: Harry Potter used this charm to cut Cedric Diggory's bag. Ron Weasley used it the second time to cut the lace from the cuffs of his dress robes because he wanted to look masculine. Harry used this charm again to swap the covers of his new and second-hand copies.

Say: dih-FIN-doh

6. Diminuendo

Classification: Charm

Interpretation: This charm causes shrinkage of the target.

Seen/Specified: Nigel Wolpert performed it in 1995.

Say: dim-in-YEW-en-DOUGH

7. Dissendium

Classification: Charm

Interpretation: This spell opens secret passages as well as general objects.

Seen/Specified: The Statue of Gunhilda of Gorsemoor was opened by this spell in 1993. Four years later, it was used to open Salazar Slytherin's Locket, but it was a failed attempt.

Say: dih-SEN-dee-um

Notes: This may not be a spell in the strict sense at all, but a password; however, when you use a hunchback witch statue, you need to tap the statue with your wand, indicating that it is, in fact, a spell.

8. Draconifors

Classification: Transfiguration

Interpretation: This spell changes the target into a dragon.

Spell class: Draconifors Spell

Say: drah-KOH-nih-fors

9. Ducklifors

Classification: Jinx, Transfiguration

Interpretation: In 1994 and 1995, this spell was frequently used.

Spell class: Ducklifors Jinx

Seen/Specified: This spell was used many times in 1994 , 1995.

Say: DUCK-lih-fors

10. Duro

Classification: Charm

Interpretation: This charm changes the target into a stone.

Spell class: Hardening Charm

Seen/Specified: Hermione Granger used this spell in 1998 while getting away from the Death Eaters in the Battle of Hogwarts.

Say: DYOO-roh

E

1. Ebublio

Classification: Jinx

Interpretation: This is a jinx, which changes the victim into hundreds of bubbles. An ally is needed to use Aqua Eructo on the victim while the jinx is being spelled.

Spell class: Ebublio Jinx

Seen/Specified: This jinx was used in 1994.

Say: ee-BUB-lee-oh

2. Engorgio

Classification: Charm

Interpretation: This charm is the opposite of the shrink charm and causes the victim to swell in physical size.

Spell class: Engorgement Charm

Seen/Specified: In 1992, this spell was used by Rubeus Hagrid on his pumpkins. Barty Crouch Jr used it two years later to cast this spell on a spider. He did this to assist students.

Say: en-GOR-jee-oh

3. Engorgio Skullus

Classification: Hex

Interpretation: This hex results in the swelling of the skull of the victim. This hex has a counter-hex, which is Redactum Skullus. The counter-hex causes a decrease in swelling.

Seen/Specified: Wiseacre's Wizarding Equipment in Diagon Alley sell this spell.

Say: in-GORE-jee-oh SKUH-las

4. Entomorphis

Classification: Transfiguration, Jinx

Interpretation: This is a hex, which changes the target into an insect for a short period of time.

Spell class: Insect Jinx

Seen/Specified: Harry Potter was going to use it against Dudley Dursley in 1995 but decided against it.

Say: en-TOE-morph-is

5. Episkey

Classification: Healing Spell

Interpretation: The spell is used to heal minor injuries, broken bones, and cartilage.

Seen/Specified: Nymphadora Tonks used it to fix Harry's wrecked nose when Draco Malfoy broke it on the Hogwarts Express in 1996. Harry used it to heal Demelza Robins' swollen lip after Ron injured her during the Quidditch rehearsal.

Say: ee-PIS-key

6. Epoximise

Classification: Transfiguration

Interpretation: This spell is used to fix or glue two objects with one another.

Seen/Specified: Students often used this spell to adhere each other's hand or belongings in the school.

Say: ee-POX-i-mise

7. Erecto

Classification: Charm

Interpretation: This spell is used to erect tents or other structures that have an upright position.

Seen/Specified: Hermione Granger used this charm to build a safe place for herself, Harry, and Ronald in 1997.

Say: eh-RECK-toh

8. Evanesce

Classification: Transfiguration

Interpretation: This spell is used to make the target disappear.

Say: eh-RECK-toh

9. Evanesco

Classification: Transfiguration

Interpretation: This spell makes the target disappear permanently.

Spell class: Vanishing Spell

Seen/Specified: William Weasley used this spell to make a bundle of old scrolls disappear whilst cleaning 12 Grimmauld Place in 1995.

Say: ev-an-ES-koh

10. Everte Statum

Classification: Spell

Interpretation: This spell acts as a push and throws the target backwards.

Seen/Specified: This spell was used by Draco Malfoy on HP in 1992 during the Duelling Club.

Say: ee-VER-tay STAH-tum

11. Expecto Patronum

Classification: Charm

Interpretation: This is a powerful charm, which conjures a guardian of the person that protects him from dark creatures. The guardian is in the shape of an animal, depending upon the characteristics and emotions of the person who casts it. With the change in emotions of the caster, the form of his guardian's animal changes as well.

Seen/Specified: Remus Lupin taught Harry Potter this charm during his Anti-Dementor lessons. Harry Potter later taught Dumbledore's Army. Dementors or Lethifolds can face an effective opposition due to this charm.

Say: ecks-PECK-toh pah-TROH-numb

12. Expelliarmus

Classification: Charm

Interpretation: Considered Harry's signature spell, it can force anything out of the hand of the target.

Seen/Specified: Severus Snape used this spell on Gilderoy Lockhart during a live duelling demonstration between the first and last meeting of the Duelling Club in 1992.

Say: ex-PELL-ee-ARE-muss

F

1. Ferula

Classification: Healing spell, Conjuration

Interpretation: This spell fixes the bandages around the wounds of the target.

Spell class: Bandaging Charm

Seen/Specified: In 1994, Remus Lupin used this spell to bind Ronald Weasley's broken leg.

Say: fer-ROOL-lah

2. Fianto Duri

Classification: Charm

Interpretation: It is a defensive charm that strengthens shield spells and other things in general.

Seen/Specified: This spell was used to protect Hogwarts in 1998.

Say: fee-AN-toh DOO-ree

3. Finestra

Classification: Charm

Interpretation: Breaks glass in pieces.

Spell class: Finestra spell

Seen/Specified: On 6 December 1926, Newt Scamander broke the front window of the Voclain & Co. jewellery store using this spell. He was trying to recapture his niffler.

Say: fi-NESS-tra

4. Finite Incantatem

Classification: Counter-Spell

Interpretation: This spell keeps the caster safe from spells in the surroundings.

Spell class: General Counter-Spell

Seen/Specified: Used by Severus Snape to restore order to the Duelling Club in 1992 while there was chaos in the event.

Say: fi-NEE-tay in-can-TAH-tem

5. Flagrate

Classification: Charm

Interpretation: This charm is used to write in the air.

Seen/Specified: Used by Tom Riddle to write his name. Used by Hermione Granger, three years later, to mark some doors.

Say: flah-GRAH-tay

6. Flintifors

Type: Transfiguration
Pronunciation: FLINT–i–fors
Description: Transforms objects into matchboxes.

SPELL HP

7. Flipendo

Classification: Jinx

Interpretation: Pushes the target backwards.

Spell class: Knockback Jinx

Seen/Specified: Defence Against the Dark Arts taught this jinx. Every video game used it thereafter until the third one.

Say: fli-PEN-doh

8. Flipendo Duo

Classification: Jinx

Interpretation: Flipendo's powerful version.

Spell class: Knockback Jinx Duo

Seen/Specified: This jinx was seen in 1991, 1992, and 1993.

Say: flih-PEN-doh DOO-oh

9. Fumos

Classification: Charm

Interpretation: This charm causes a smoky screen, which reduces visibility.

Spell class: Smokescreen Spell

Seen/Specified: This spell was used in 1993 and is covered in The Dark Forces: A Guide to Self-Protection.

Say: FYOO-moss

10. Furnunculus

Classification: Jinx

Interpretation: This jinx con covers the target in pimples.

Seen/Specified: It was used by Harry Potter on Gregory Goyle.

Say: fer-NUN-kyoo-luss

1. Geminio (Doubling Charm)

Type: Charm

Pronunciation: jeh-MIH-nee-oh

Description: Duplicates the target. When used to duplicate objects indefinitely on purpose, is known as the Gemino Curse.

SPELL HP

2. Glacius

Classification: Charm

Interpretation: This spell covers the target in cold air and freezes them.

Seen/Specified: This charm has been used in the video games, starting from Harry Potter and the Prisoner of Azkaban (video game).

Say: GLAY-see-us

3. Glisseo

Classification: Charm

Interpretation: Changes the steps of a stair into a flat slide.

Seen/Specified: Hermione Granger used this spell to escape from the Death Eaters.

Say: GLISS-ee-oh

H

1. Harmonia Nectere Passus

Classification: Charm

Interpretation: This spell can repair a cabinet that starts vanishing.

Seen/Specified: Draco Malfoy used this spell to mend a cabinet in 1996.

Say: har-MOH-nee-a_NECK-teh-ray_PASS-us

2. Herbifors

Classification: Transfiguration

Interpretation: Flowers start sprouting from the body of the victim.

3. Herbivicus

Classification: Charm

Interpretation: Increases the growth of plants.

Spell class: Herbivicus Charm

Seen/Specified: Was seen in the 1994–1995 school year.

Say: her-BIV-i-cuss

4. Homenum Revelio

Classification: Charm

Interpretation: The caster gets to know the presence of any human around.

Spell class: Human-Presence-Revealing Spell

Seen/Specified: This spell was used multiple times by various people in 1997.

Say: HOM-eh-num reh-VEH-lee-oh

I

1. Illegibilus

Classification: Charm

Interpretation: Turns writing into non-readable.

Say: i-LEDJ-i-bull-is

2. Immobulus

Classification: Charm

Interpretation: It stops the actions of the target. The target can be both living or non-living.

Seen/Specified: This spell was used by Hermione in 1992 to freeze two Cornish Pixies.

Say: ih-MOH-byoo-luhs

3. Impedimenta

Classification: Jinx

Interpretation: Reduces the speed of the target and eventually stops it.

Seen/Specified: Harry Potter used it in 1995 while he was practicing.

Say: im-ped-ih-MEN-tah

4. Imperio

Classification: Curse

Interpretation: The victim comes under the control of the caster. This spell turns the victim into a slave as he starts to obey the orders of the caster. Some people may learn to resist this spell.

Spell class: Imperius Curse

Seen/Specified: Used on many occasions. In 1994, the spell was used when Barty Crouch Jr, impersonating ex-Auror Alastor Moody, used it on a spider and later on, students used it during a "class march" in a Defence Against the Dark Arts class. Harry used this spell on Goblin as well.

Say: im-PEER-ee-oh

4. Impervius

Classification: Charm

Interpretation: The target starts repelling mist and water.

Spell class: Impervius Charm

Seen/Specified: Hermione Granger used this spell in 1993 on Harry's glasses while in a Quidditch match and also by the Gryffindor Quidditch team. This spell was used in 1997, first by Ron to protect objects in Yaxley's office from rain, and then by Hermione to defend Harry, Ron and Griphook from the scorching treasure in the Lestranges' vault.

Say: im-PUR-vee-us

5. Incarcerous

Classification: Conjuration

Interpretation: This spell ties the target with ropes of thin air.

Seen/Specified: Dolores Umbridge tries to hold off Centaurs in 1996 for the first time. Also used by Harry on the Inferi in Voldemort's Crystal Cave and also tried to use it on Severus Snape in 1997.

Say: in-KAR-ser-us

6. Incendio

Classification: Conjuration, Charm

Interpretation: This spell results in the production of fire.

Seen/Specified: Arthur Weasley used it in 1997 to create a fire in the Dursleys' hearth to use Floo powder there. In 1997, this spell was used many times in fights, most noticeably when Hagrid's hut was set on fire.

Say: in-SEN-dee-oh

7. Inflatus (Inflating Charm)

Type: Charm
Pronunciation: in-FLAY-tus
Description: Inflates the target, filling it with air.

SPELL HP

L

1. Locomotor Wibbly

Classification: Jinx, Curse

Interpretation: This spell results in the collapsing of the legs of the victim as if they were made of jelly or other soft material.

Spell class: Jelly-Legs Curse

Seen/Specified: Harry used this jinx, and Draco was hit by this jinx.

Say: loh-koh-MOH-tor WIB-lee

2. Lacarnum Inflamari

Classification: Charm

Interpretation: Cloaks of the target catches fire.

Seen/Specified: Hermione used it in 1991 to stop Snape from cursing Harry. This one is only used in the films.

Say: la-KAR-num in-flah-MAR-ee

3. Langlock

Classification: Jinx

Interpretation: The target can't speak due to the failure to move his/her tongue.

Seen/Specified: Harry used it on Peeves and twice on Argus Filch to general ovation.

Say: LANG-lock

4. Legilimens

Classification: Charm

Interpretation: The caster gets into the mind of the target and can read thoughts and emotions.

Seen/Specified: Severus Snape used it on Harry after he had a dream about Arthur Weasley being attacked by Nagini in 1995. Occlumency lessons in 1996 were also accompanied by the use of this spell. Also used non-verbally by Snape on Harry in 1997 to let him to see where Harry had cultured the Sectumsempra spell.

Say: Le-JIL-ih-mens

5. Levicorpus

Classification: Jinx

Interpretation: People get stuck in the air by their ankle. Severus Snape created this spell.

Seen/Specified: The Half-Blood Prince invented it, and it is a non-verbal-only. Harry Potter learnt it from the readings and notes written by the Half-Blood Prince. He used it on Ron to test it. The previous year, Harry had seen his father, James Potter, who used the spell against Professor Snape.

Say: leh-vee-COR-pus

6. Liberacorpus

Classification: Counter-Jinx

Interpretation: This jinx is a counter-jinx to Levicorpus.

Seen/Specified: It was used by Harry in 1996 to counteract Levicorpus that he had unintentionally cast on Ron.

Say: LIB-er-ah-cor-pus

7. Locomotor

Classification: Charm

Interpretation: This spell is used to move objects which are targeted by the caster. The extent of movement is not much, but it moves them a few inches. The spell is said before the name of the object, which is to be moved.

Seen/Specified: Nymphadora Tonks used this spell in Harry Potter to move Harry's trunk from his room. Filius Flitwick also tried it to move Sybill Trelawney's trunk after Dolores Umbridge sacked her.

Say: loh-kuh-MOH-tor

8. Locomotor Mortis

Classification: Curse

Interpretation: Binds the legs without anything.

Spell class: Leg-Locker Curse

Seen/Specified: Draco Malfoy used it on Neville Longbottom in 1991. Harry Potter used it on Draco Malfoy, who rebounded it in 1996. One of the spells on Pottermore.

Say: LOH-koh-moh-tor MOR-tis

9. Lumos

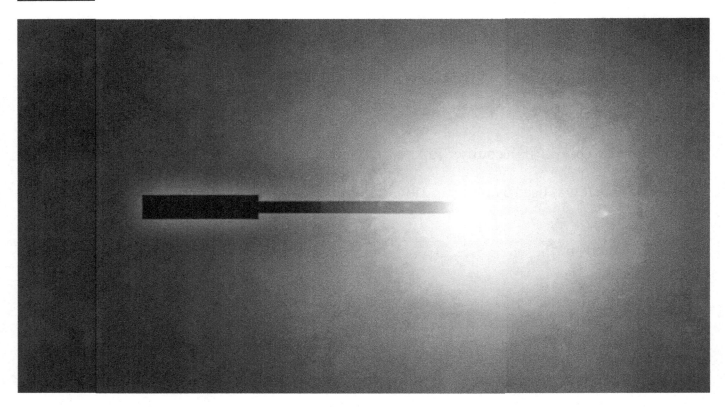

Classification: Charm

Interpretation: Turns the wand of the caster into a torch, which can be used to light dark places.

Spell class: Wand-Lighting Charm

Seen/Specified: This spell has been used throughout the film when there is a need for light in any dark place.

Say: LOO-mos

10. Lumos Solem

Classification: Charm

Interpretation: This spell can result in the production of a blinding flash of sunlight. It is a modified form of the Wand-Lighting Charm.

Seen/Specified: Hermione used this to free Ron from the Devil's Snare. The chant was only used in the film variation of Harry Potter and the Philosopher's Stone.

Say: LOO-mos SO-lem

M

1. Melofors

Classification: Jinx

Interpretation: The head of the victim gets stuck into a pumpkin.

Spell class: Melofors Jinx

Seen/Specified: Cornelius Fudge was thought to be the victim of this spell.

2. Meteolojinx Recanto

Classification: Counter-Charm

Interpretation: This counter-charm stops the weather effects, which are caused by jinxes.

Seen/Specified: Suggested in 1997 by Arthur Weasley to Ron that this jinx was the best way to clear the rain jinxes at the Ministry offices. ABartemius Crouch Jr (disguised as Alastor Moody) used this spell in 1994 to stop the weather effect of the Great Hall's Ceiling because he said it is broken, and Dumbledore should "Fix his ceiling."

Say: mee-tee-OH-loh-jinks reh-CAN-toh.

3. Mimblewimble

Classification: Curse

Interpretation: This spell ties the tongue of the target and makes it harder for them to chant or spell against the caster. It is very useful against a powerful witch or wizard.

Spell class: Tongue-Tying Curse

Seen/Specified: This spell was seen in 1997 as a deterrent to Severus Snape, who was a capable speller, or any other visitor who was not wanted at 12 Grimmauld Place, from revealing their location to anyone else.

Say: MIM-bull-wim-bull

4. Mobiliarbus

Classification: Charm

Interpretation: This charm is used to move wooden objects only. It can move those objects a few inches and can draw them in any direction.

Seen/Specified: Hermione Granger used the spell to move a Christmas Tree in The Three Broomsticks in 1993. She did this to hide Harry Potter, who was in Hogsmeade illegally.

Say: mo-bil-lee-AR-bus

5. Mobilicorpus

Classification: Charm

Interpretation: This Charm can move the body that is targeted by the caster.

Seen/Specified: Used by Sirius Black against Severus Snape in 1994. Lord Voldemort used it on Peter Pettigrew in the graveyard to make him come forward.

Say: moh-bil-lee-COR-pus

6. Molliare

Classification: Charm

Interpretation: This spell can produce a cushion, which is invisible and over the target. Basically, this spell is used to manufacture the broomsticks.

Spell class: Cushioning Charm

Seen/Specified: Hermione Granger used this spell to cushion her, Harry, and Ron's fall in Gringotts Wizard Bank in 1998.

Say: mull-ee-AR-ay

7. Morsmordre

Interpretation: This spell can conjure the Dark Mark on the target. Dark Mark is the sign of the Death Eaters.

Seen/Specified: Barty Crouch Jr used this spell in 1994. This spell was also seen in 1997 over the castle to trap Albus Dumbledore to his death. Lord Voldemort invented it.

Say: morz-MOR-druh

8. Mucus ad Nauseam

Classification: Curse

Interpretation: This spell gives the target a very runny nose and cold. This condition can result in the collapse of the victim if the victim is not treated. Constant sneezing is also a result of this spell.

Spell class: Curse of the Bogies

Seen/Specified: Professor Quirrell mentioned it to his first-year class.

Say: MYOO-kus ahd NAW-zee-um

9. Muffliato

Classification: Charm

Interpretation: This spell causes a buzzing in the ears of people around the caster. They can't identify this buzzing and can't hear the conversations.

Spell class: Muffliato Charm

Seen/Specified: Harry Potter and Ron Weasley used it in 1996 on various teachers and people, such as Madam Pomfrey. Severus Snape created it. Hermione pointed out that it is probably not Ministry of Magic approved. Hermione Granger used it in 1997 to protect the camp-site where Harry and she stayed in hiding.

Say: muf-lee-AH-to

10. Multicorfors

Classification: Transfiguration

Interpretation: This charm is used to change the colour and style of the caster's clothing.

Spell class: Multicorfors Spell

Seen/Specified: Harry once changed the colour of his eyebrows accidentally, and then he changed the clothing of his teachers by using this charm.

Say: mull-tee-COR-fors

N

1. Nox

Classification: Charm

Interpretation: It is the counter-charm for the Wand-Lighting Charm and can darken and turn-off the illuminated wands of the target.

Spell class: Wand-Extinguishing Charm

Seen/Specified: Used by Harry Potter and Hermione Granger in 1994 to turn off their wand-lights in the Shrieking Shack. Harry used it in 1998 when he was in the passage beneath the Whomping Willow, which leads to the Shrieking Shack.

Say: NOCKSS

2. Nebulus

Classification: Charm

Interpretation: This charm can create fog from the tip of the wand of the caster.

Seen/Specified: Used by Albus Dumbledore in 1927 to conjure a fog in London to form a coverup for his meeting with Newton Scamander.

Say: NEH-bu-lus

O

1. Oculus Reparo

Classification: Charm

Interpretation: This spell is used to mend the broken eyeglasses.

Seen/Specified: Hermione used this spell in 1991 and 1992 to fix Harry's glasses.

2. Obliviate

Classification: Charm

Interpretation: This spell can erase the required memories from the brain of the target.

Spell class: Memory Charm

Seen/Specified: Gilderoy Lockhart used this spell on Harry and Ron in 1993. The spell rebounded due to a defective wand, costing Lockhart most of his own memory. Hermione Granger used this spell to remove her parents' memories in 1997. This spell was also used in 1997 by Hermione Granger on two Death Eaters.

Say: oh-BLI-vee-ate

3. Obscuro

Classification: Conjuration

Interpretation: The target is blindfolded by this spell.

Seen/Specified: Hermione Granger used this spell in 1997. The purpose was to obstruct the portrait of Phineas Nigellus's view of their location.

Say: ob-SKYUR-oh

4. Oppugno

Classification: Jinx

Interpretation: This spell can make the targeted objects attack the victim The caster can use this with other spells during a fight.

Spell class: Oppugno Jinx

Seen/Specified: Hermione Granger used this spell in 1996 to attack Ron Weasley with a summoned flock of canaries during an argument between both of them.

Say: oh-PUG-noh

5. Orbis

Classification: Jinx

Interpretation: This spell can result in the sucking of the target by the ground.

Spell class: Orbix Jinx

Seen/Specified: This spell was seen multiple times during 1993.

Say: OR-biss

6. Orchideous

Classification: Conjuration

Interpretation: This spell is used for conjuring a bouquet of flowers.

Seen/Specified: Mr. Ollivander used it in 1994 to test Fleur Delacour's wand. Riddle used this spell to present flowers to Mrs. Smith.

Say: or-KID-ee-us

7. Oscausi

Classification: Dark charm

Interpretation: This spell seals the mouth of the target in such a way that it seems that there was no mouth on the target's face.

Seen/Specified: Leta Lestrange used this spell on a girl from Gryffindor when they were both in their third year at Hogwarts. The Gryffindor girl was speaking ill of Lestrange behind her back until Lestrange came on the scene and used this spell to mute the other girl.

Say: os-SCOW-zee

P

1. Pack

Classification: Charm

Interpretation: This spell packs the luggage of the caster.

Seen/Specified: Remus Lupin used this spell in Harry Potter and the Prisoner of Azkaban in his office, and in Harry Potter and the Order of the Phoenix by Nymphadora Tonks, once orally and again, non-verbally.

2. Papyrus Reparo

Classification: Charm

Interpretation: This charm mends pieces of paper.

Seen/Specified: Newton Scamander used this spell in 1927 to restore a torn postcard from Porpentina Goldstein, which was sent to Queenie Goldstein.

3. Partis Temporus

Classification: Charm

Interpretation: This spell can create an impermanent gap in the target.

Seen/Specified: Albus Dumbledore used this spell in the Crystal Cave in the film adaptation of Harry Potter and the Half-Blood Prince. He used it so that he and Harry could easily pass through the ring of fire used to ward off the Inferi.

Say: PAR-tis temp-OAR-us

4. Periculum

Classification: Charm

Interpretation: Red sparks are produced by this charm.

Seen/Specified: Harry used this charm during the third task of the Tri-wizard Tournament.

Say: pur-ICK-you-lum

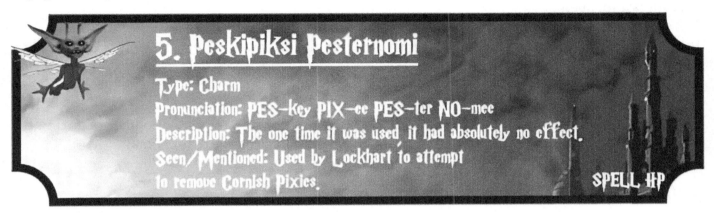

5. Peskipiksi Pesternomi

Type: Charm

Pronunciation: PES-key PIX-ee PES-ter NO-mee

Description: The one time it was used, it had absolutely no effect.

Seen/Mentioned: Used by Lockhart to attempt to remove Cornish Pixies.

SPELL, HP

6. Petrificus Totalus

Classification: Curse

Interpretation: This spell binds the body of the victim as if it is a soldier, and it falls on the ground at the end.

Spell class: Full Body-Bind Curse

Seen/Specified: Hermione used it in 1991 and was trying to prevent Neville from stopping her, Ron, and Harry from getting out of the common room to hunt for the Philosopher's Stone. This was used in the Hall of Prophecy in the film adaptation of Harry Potter and the Order of the Phoenix to terrify one of the Death Eaters following the group, and was used on Harry by Draco Malfoy in the train in 'Harry Potter and the Half-Blood Prince.

Say: pe-TRI-fi-cus to-TAH-lus

7. Piertotum Locomotor

Classification: Charm

Interpretation: This spell can animate inanimate targets during a fight.

Seen/Specified: In the Battle of Hogwarts, Professor McGonagall used this spell to bring to life and fight. The objects were the suits of armour and sculptures within Hogwarts to protect the castle. Albus Dumbledore used this to enchant the statues on the fountain in the entrance to the Ministry of Magic Department.

Say: peer-TOH-tuhm loh-kuh-MOH-tor

8. Point Me

Classification: Spell

Interpretation: This spell helps the caster in knowing the direction. The wand points to the north.

Spell class: Four-Point Spell

Seen/Specified: Harry Potter was taught this spell by Hermione Granger, who used it during the Triwizard Tournament, chiefly to navigate the hedge maze during the Third Task.

9. Portus

Classification: Charm

Interpretation: The object is turned into a portkey by this spell.

Seen/Specified: Albus Dumbledore used this spell in 1996.

Say: POR-tus

10. Prior Incantato

Classification: Charm

Interpretation: This spell forces the wand to show the echo of the last spell that was performed by it.

Spell class: Reverse Spell

Seen/Specified: Amos Diggory used this spell in 1994 to see the last spell cast by Harry's wand after it was found in the hands of Winky, a house-elf.

Say: pri-OR in-can-TAH-toh

11. Protego

Classification: Charm

Interpretation: An invisible shield is formed by the spell that can reflect spells and block physical entities.

Spell class: Shield Charm

Seen/Specified: Harry is taught this spell by Hermione in 1995 during his preparation for the third task in the Triwizard Tournament. Albus Dumbledore used a similar spell, which turns the building of glass back into the form of sand when Voldemort sent the remains of glass to try to stab Dumbledore.

Say: pro-TAY-goh

12. Protego Diabolica

Classification: Dark Arts

Interpretation: A ring of black fire is formed around the caster, and it keeps the caster safe from enemies.

Say: pro-TAY-goh dia-BOHL-i-cub

13. Protego Horribilis

Classification: Charm

Interpretation: This is a shield charm against dark magic and protects the caster.

Seen/Specified: Professor Flitwick cast this in an attempt to strengthen the castle's defences in the Battle of Hogwarts.

Say: pro-TAY-goh horr-uh-BIHL-ihs

14. Protego Totalum

Classification: Charm

Interpretation: This is also a shield charm, which protects the area for a long period of time.

Seen/Specified: Hermione Granger and Harry Potter used it in 1997 to protect their campsite from unwanted visitors.

Say: pro-TAY-goh toh-TAH-lum

Q

1. Quietus

Classification: Charm

Interpretation: It is the counter-charm to the Amplifying Charm, and it makes the target sound quieter.

Spell class: Quietening Charm

Seen/Specified: Ludo Bagman used it in 1994.

Say: KWIY-uh-tus

R

1. Redactum Skullus

Classification: Hex

Interpretation: It is the counter-spell to Engorgio Skullus, and this spell shrinks the head of the target.

Spell class: Head Shrink Spell

Say: reh-DAK-tum SKULL-us

2. Reducio

Classification: Charm

Interpretation: Its counter-charm is the Engorgement Charm, and this spell can shrink the physical size of the targeted object.

Spell class: Shrinking Charm

Seen/Specified: Harry Potter checked his Blackthorn wand on the Bluebell flames with Engorgio, casting this spell to shorten the size of flames, which were previously enlarged.

Say: re-DOO-see-oh

3. Reducto

Classification: Curse

Interpretation: This spell can break or disintegrate the targeted object into pieces.

Spell class: Reductor Curse

Seen/Specified: Used by Harry in 1995 on one of the hedges of the Triwizard maze and ends up burning a small hole in it. Gryffindors in Harry Potter's year gave the reference of Parvati Patil as being able to reduce a table full of Dark Detectors to ashes, and Harry and his friends later used the spell in the Department of Mysteries against the Death Eaters, breaking many Prophecy Orbs in the process.

Say: re-DUK-toh

4. Reparifors

Classification: Healing Spell

Interpretation: This spell can revert small ailments induced by magic, such as paralysis and poisoning.

Seen/Specified: This spell is seen in Harry Potter and the Prisoner of Azkaban (video game).

Say: re-PAR-i-fors

5. Relashio

Classification: Jinx

Interpretation: This spell is used to loosen the grip of the target on whatever it is holding.

Spell class: Revulsion Jinx

Seen/Specified: Harry Potter used this spell against Grindylows in the second task of the Triwizard Tournament. Hermione used this spell to free Mrs. Cattermole from the chained chair and to free the Ukrainian Ironbelly in 1997 and 1998.

Say: ruh-LASH-ee-oh

6. Rennervate

Classification: Charm

Interpretation: It is consequently the counter-charm to the Stunning Spell, and this spell can awaken a victim who is not conscious.

Seen/Specified: Amos Diggory used it in 1994 to wake up Winky, and Albus Dumbledore used it to wake up Viktor Krum.

Say: RENN-a-vate

7. Reparo

Classification: Charm

Interpretation: This spell can perfectly repair broken objects.

Spell class: Mending Charm

Seen/Specified: The series contains a lot of events where this spell is being used. Harry smashed a bowl of murtlap essence in 1995. He could repair the bowl, but the murtlap essence remained scattered on the floor.

Say: reh-PAH-roh

8. Repello Muggletum

Classification: Charm

Interpretation: This charm keeps the muggles away as it makes them forget their purpose, and they get confused.

Say: ruh-PEL-oh MUH-guhl-tuhm

9. Repello Inimicum

Classification: Charm

Interpretation: Anyone who enters into this charm disintegrates into pieces.

Seen/Specified: Filius Flitwick and Horace Slughorn, along with Order of the Phoenix member, Molly Weasley, used this spell to safeguard Hogwarts Castle in 1998.

Say: re-PEH-lloh ee-nee-MEE-cum

10. Revelio

Classification: Charm

Interpretation: This spell reveals the secrets of any object or person.

Say: reh-VEL-ee-oh

11. Rictusempra

Classification: Charm

Interpretation: This charm tickles the target so much that it becomes weak with laughter.

Seen/Specified: This spell was used by Harry Potter on Draco Malfoy in 1992 when they quarreled in the Duelling Club.

Say: ric-tuhs-SEM-pra

12. Riddikulus

Classification: Charm

Interpretation: A spell used when fighting a Boggart, "Riddikulus" forces the Boggart to take the appearance of an object the caster is focusing on. Best results can be achieved if the caster is focusing on something humorous, with the desire that laughter will weaken the Boggart.

Seen/Specified: Taught by Remus Lupin during third year Defence Against the Dark Arts, where his students had the opportunity to practise the spell on an actual Boggart.

Say: rih-dih-KUL-lus

S

1. Salvio Hexia

Classification: Charm

Interpretation: This charm protects the caster against hexes.

Seen/Specified: In 1997, Harry and Hermione cast this spell to strengthen their campsite's defences against burglars.

Say: SAL-vee-oh HECKS-ee-ah

2. Scourgify

Classification: Charm

Interpretation: This spell helps in cleaning objects.

Spell class: Scouring Charm

Seen/Specified: Nymphadora Tonks used this spell for the first time to clean Hedwig's cage in 1995. Ginny Weasley also performed the spell to clean up the Stinksap on the Hogwarts Express.

Say: SKUR-ji-fy

3. Sectumsempra

Classification: Curse

Interpretation: This curse kills the target due to bleeding as the target is lacerated. Severus Snape used this spell against their personal enemies.

Seen/Specified: Harry used this curse in 1997 against Draco Malfoy, and then later against both the Inferi in Lord Voldemort's Horcrux chamber. On the other hand, Snape used it on his enemy George Weasley in the Order's flight from Privet Drive. Harry came to know about these from Snape's textbooks. This spell is known as a signature spell of Snape.

Say: sec-tum-SEMP-rah

4. Serpensortia

Classification: Conjuration

Interpretation: A snake comes out of the wand of the caster.

Seen/Specified: Draco Malfoy used this spell while duelling with Harry Potter in 1992.

Say: ser-pen-SOR-shah, SER-pehn-SOR-tee-ah

5. Silencio

Classification: Charm

Interpretation: This spell is used to make something silent.

Spell class: Silencing Charm

Seen/Specified: Hermione used it for the first time in 1996 to silence a frog and a raven in Charms class. Later, it was used to silence a Death Eater that was trying to tell his comrades where they were.

Say: sih-LEN-see-oh

6. Sonorus

Classification: Charm

Interpretation: This charm increases the sound of the target.

Spell class: Amplifying Charm

Seen/Specified: Ludo Bagman used this charm in 1994 at the beginning of the Quidditch World Cup. Albus Dumbledore used it several times in the Triwizard Championship. Lord Voldemort used this charm several times during the Battle of Hogwarts in 1998.

Say: soh-NOHR-uhs

7. Specialis Revelio

Classification: Charm

Interpretation: This spell reveals spells cast on objects or potions.

Seen/Specified: Hermione Granger used this spell to find out more about Harry's Advanced Potion-Making book in 1996. Ernie Macmillan used this spell to find out the ingredients of a potion.

Say: spe-see-AL-is reh-VEL-ee-oh

8. Steleus

Classification: Hex

Interpretation: This is a hex that causes distraction as it causes sneeze in the target.

Say: STEH-lee-us

9. Stupefy

Classification: Charm

Interpretation: The target stays stunned as if unconscious.

Spell class: Stunning Spell

Seen/Specified: A number of wizards and witches used this charm against Minerva McGonagall in 1996. Harry taught this spell in his D.A. Meetings.

Say: STOO-puh-fye

10. Surgito

Classification: Counter-charm

Interpretation: This is a counter-charm and is often used to to remove enchantments.

Seen/Specified: Used by Newton Scamander in 1927 to lift an enchantment that was placed on Jacob Kowalski.

Say: SUR-jee-toh

T

1. Tarantallegra

Classification: Jinx

Interpretation: Target starts dancing uncontrollably.

Seen/Specified: Draco Malfoy on Harry Potter for the first time in the Duelling Club in 1992.

Say: ta-RON-ta-LEG-gra

2. Tergeo

Classification: Charm

Interpretation: This spell can drain off liquid and clean objects.

Seen/Specified: Used by Hermione Granger in 1996, the spell removed blood from Harry's face. It is also used to remove dropped ink from parchment. Ron used it in 1997 to clean off a handkerchief and to dust off a picture of Gellert Grindelwald.

Say: TUR-jee-oh

3. Titillando (Tickling Hex)

Type: Hex

Pronunciation: ti-tee-LAN-do

Description: Tickles and weakens the victim.

SPELL HP

V

1. Vera Verto

Classification: Transfiguration

Interpretation: This spell turns animals into goblets.

Seen/Specified: Minerva McGonagall used it only once in the film in the adaptation of Harry Potter and the Chamber of Secrets at her Transfiguration class.

Say: vair-uh-VAIR-toh

2. Verdimillious

Classification: Charm

Interpretation: This spell produces a jet of green sparks, which can be used to trace the dark magic.

Seen/Specified: This spell was used many times from 1991 until 1994.

Say: vur-duh-MILL-ee-us

3. Verdimillious Duo

Classification: Charm

Interpretation: A more upgraded version of Verdimillious.

Seen/Specified: This charm was taught in the first-year defence against the Dark Arts class.

Say: VERD-dee-MILL-lee-us

4. Vermillious

Classification: Charm

Interpretation: This spell produced a jet of red sparks that signal an emergency or as a minor duelling spell.

Spell class: Red Sparks

Say: vur-MILL-ee-us

5. Vipera Evanesca

Classification: Vanishment

Interpretation: It is the counter-spell for the Snake Summons Spell and is used for vanishing snakes.

Spell class: Snake-Vanishing Spell

Seen/Specified: In 1992, Severus Snape cast this spell at the Duelling Club to vanish a snake that Draco Malfoy had conjured while duelling Harry Potter. This spell was also used by Albus Dumbledore to vanish Voldemort's snake during their Duel in the Ministry Atrium.

Say: vee-PAIR-uh eh-vuh-NES-kuh

6. Vulnera Sanentur

Classification: Healing Spell

Interpretation: It is the counter-curse to Sectumsempra, as it is a healing spell. It slows blood flow and heals the wounds.

Seen/Specified: Severus Snape healed the wounds of Draco Malfoy, which were caused by the Sectumsempra curse cast by Harry Potter in 1997.

Say: VUL-ner-ah sah-NEN-tour

1. Waddiwasi

Classification: Jinx

Interpretation: This is a jinx that is used to throw small objects on the target.

Seen/Specified: Remus Lupin in 1993 cast this jinx on Peeves the Poltergeist, sending a wad of chewing gum up his nose.

Say: wah-deh-WAH-see

2. Wingardium Leviosa

Classification: Charm

Interpretation: This charm makes objects fly or float in the air.

Spell class: Levitation Charm

Seen/Specified: This charm was taught in the initial charm classes, and it came into use when Ron Weasley performed a mountain troll. Harry used this charm six years later to lift the side-car of his grandfather's motorbike.

Say: win-GAR-dee-um lev-ee-OH-sa

Q. Why does Professor Snape stand in the middle of the road?

A. So you'll never know which side he's on.

JOKES HP

QUIZ

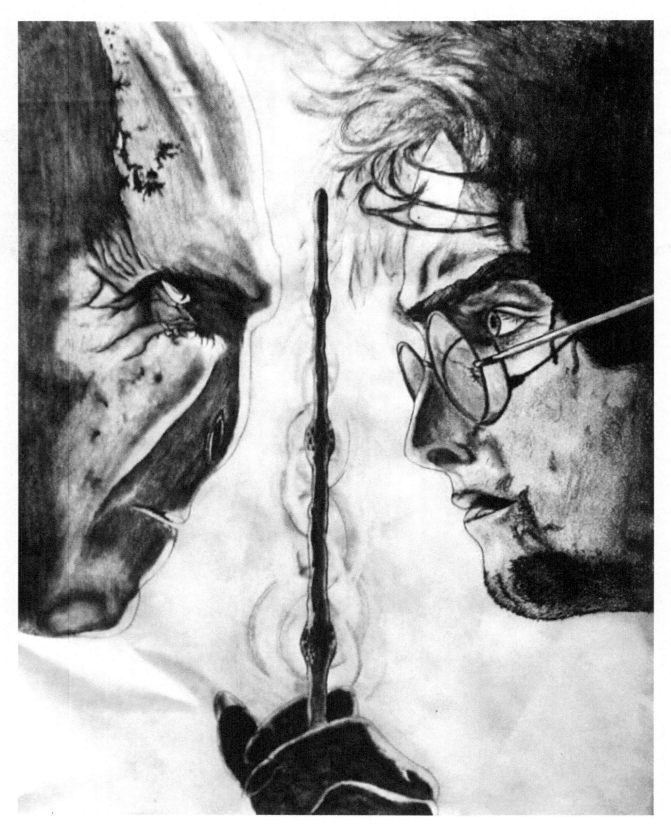

GRADE GUIDE

Follow this guide and have a swell time with your friends. And even if you want to enjoy it alone, have fun too!

This quiz comes with seven consecutive levels. And each tier comes with 30 daunting questions about wizardry.

The levels get tougher progressively. So, even if you got the hang of the first few levels, don't get too confident of passing the others also!

If you get one answer correct, you get one point. But that's not all; some questions have more than a point. So, eventually, you can get more than 30 points in one level.

There is a marking guide at the end of every level, where you can rate yourself with the individual points you get. Another section below also contains the scoreboard, where you can write your results. You can also draw the table out on a piece of paper.

If you have the most points, you will be crowned the winner.

The pass grades are given as:

1. Outstanding (O): <28
2. Exceeds Expectations (E): 25-27
3. Acceptable (A): 20-24

The fail grades are given as:

4. Poor (P): 15-19
5. Dreadful (D): 9-14
6. Troll (T): <9

QUIZ STATISTICS

This quiz has over 700 participants.

Interesting facts

➢ Only 2% of participants could attain an "O" grade 7 times

➢ 6% of players could be rated "O" 6 times

➢ 17% of participants could get a rating of "O" 5 times

➢ About 5% of players could be rated "O" in the sixth level, which was technically the most difficult for most participants.

➢ In each level, about 43% of players could pass with a minimum rating of "A."

➢ Participants preferred the "Remus Lupin" level to the other levels

➢ 8% of the players got a "T" grade at least three times

➢ Almost all participants felt the urge to go back to read or watch the Harry Potter series again.

Harry Potter

Scoreboard

Name	Evaluation							
	Level 1	Level 2	Level 3	Level 4	Level 5	Level 6	Level 7	Result

See, for example

Name	Evaluation							
	Level 1	Level 2	Level 3	Level 4	Level 5	Level 6	Level 7	Result
LEE JORDAN	28 O	25 E	26 E	23 A	29 O	10 D	19 P	160

TRIVIA LEVEL ONE. TROLL

1) How many points does catching the Golden Snitch earn?

a. 100

b. 50

c. 120

d. 150

2) What name was Voldemort born with?

a. Alastor Moody

b. Sirius Black

c. Tom Riddle

d. Bartemius Crouch

3) What are the three types of wizard coins in order of value?

a. Knut, Sickle, Galleon

b. Denarius, Knut, Galleon

c. Galleon, Cent, Penny

d. Galleon, Ducat, Sickle

4) What is the position at Hogwarts is cursed?

a. Defense Against the Dark Arts

b. Transfiguration

c. Herbology

d. Divination

5) How many brothers did Ron Weasley have?

a. 5

b. 6

c. 7

d. 4

6) What is the name of Harry Potter's pet owl?

a. Errol

b. Hermes

c. Pigwidgeon

d. Hedwig

7) What lies at the core Harry Potters wand?

a. Unicorn tail hair

b. Dragon heartstring

c. Phoenix feather

d. Basilisk horn

8) What animal is depicted on the Hufflepuff house emblem?

a. Lion

b. Badger

c. Snake

d. Eagle

9) Who is the Slytherin house ghost?

a. Bloody Baron

b. Fat Friar

c. Sir Nicholas de Mimsy Porpington

d. Myrtle Warren

10) What spell does Harry Potter use to drive away Dementors?

a. Accio

b. Confundo

c. Crucio

d. Expecto Patronum

11) Who gave Harry the Marauder map?

a. Albus Dumbledore

b. Cedric Diggory

c. Fred and George Weasley

d. Sirius Black

12) What spell will help you disarm opponent?

a. Oculus Reparo

b. Morsmordre

c. Alohomora

d. Expelliarmus

13) What is the platform that Harry had to get the Hogwarts express from?

a. Nine and three quarters

b. Five and three quarters

c. Seven and three quarters

d. Nine and two quarters

14) What color does the death spell have?

a. Dark

b. Green

c. Blue

d. Red

15) What subject did Rubeus Hagrid teach at Hogwarts?

a. Transfiguration

b. Care of Magical Creatures

c. Herbology

d. Defence Against the Dark Arts

16) What is the name of a sweets shop near Hogwarts?

a. Scrivenshaft

b. The Three Broomsticks

c. Honeydukes

d. Hog's Head Inn

17) What does Dumbledore leave Ron in his will?

a. Snitch

b. The Tales of Beedle The Bard

c. Deluminator

d. Medallion

18) At what store does Harry Potter get his wand?

a. Ollivanders

b. Knockturn Alley

c. Gringotts

d. The Leaky Cauldron

19) Where does Dumbledore keep his memories?

a. Notepad

b. Sorting Hat

c. Deluminator

d. Pensieve

20) What device helped Hermione in The prisoner of Azkaban to be in several classes at the same

time?

a. Enchanted clock

b. Time-turner

c. Seeker

d. Broom

21) Who teaches Harry how to play Wizard's chess?

a. Hagrid

b. Dudley

c. Ron

d. Hermione

22) When is Harry Potter's birthday?

a. July 31

b. June 31

c. August 31

d. December 31

23) Which of these spells is an Unforgivable Curse?

a. Crucio

b. Stupefy

c. Impervius

d. Sectumsempra

24) Who teaches A History of Magic at Hogwarts?

a. Gilderoy Lockhart

b. Septima Vector

c. Filius Flitwick

d. Cuthbert Binns

25) Which of the following is not a feature of Slytherin house?

a. Cunning

b. Wit

c. Determination

d. Ambition

26) Who wasn't at the Dursleys ' the night Harry's parents died?

a. Sirius Black

b. Minerva McGonagall

c. Rubeus Hagrid

d. Albus Dumbledore

27) All but one of the Weasley children are at Gryffindor?

a. False

b. True

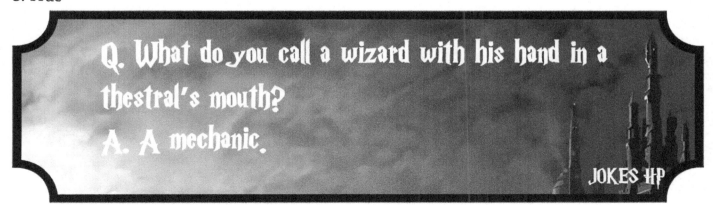

28) Whose words are those?: "I am good looking enough for both of us."

a. Gilderoy Lockhart

b. Fleur Delacour

c. Hermione Granger

d. Ron Weasley

29) Vernon and Petunia Dursley-not Harry's own uncle and aunt?

a. False

b. True

30) James Potter's nickname was Prongs?

a. True

b. False

LEVEL ONE ANSWERS

1. ➤ d) 150

2. ➤ c) Tom Riddle

3. ➤ a) Knut, Sickle, Galleon

4. ➤ a) Defense Against the Dark Arts

5. ➤ a) 5

6. ➤ d) Hedwig

7. ➤ c) Phoenix feather

8. ➤ b) Badger

9. ➤ a) Bloody Baron

10. ➤ d) Expecto Patronum

11. ➤ c) Fred and George Weasley

12. ➤ d) Expelliarmus

13. ➤ a) Nine and three quarters

14. ➤ b) Green

15. ➤ b) Care of Magical Creatures

16. ➤ c) Honeydukes

17. ➤ c) Deluminator

18. ➤ a) Ollivanders

19. ➤ d) Pensieve

20. ➤ b) Time-turner

21. ➤ c) Ron

22. ➤ a) July 31

23. ➤ a) Crucio

24. ➤ d) Cuthbert Binns

25. ➤ b) Wit

26. ➤ a) Sirius Black

27. ➤ a) False

28. ➤ b) Fleur Delacour

29. ➤ a) False

30. ➤ a) True

Interesting Facts Part One

• Rowling and Harry have the same birthday: the 31st of July.

• The Hogwarts school had six grades, divided into pass grades and the failing grades. The pass grades include Outstanding, Exceeds Expectations, and Acceptable. While the failing grades include Poor, Dreadful, and Troll.

• Ron, Harry, and Hermione all started school in 1991.

• To watch all of Harry Potter's movies at once, one would take about 18 hours, 20 minutes.

• J.K. Rowling mentioned that she just got the idea of Harry Potter one day on a train delay. She had waited for hours when the idea came to her.

TRIVIA LEVEL TWO. WEASLEY TWINS

1) What kind of animal does Hermione become when when she takes Polyjuice Potion in Chamber of Secrets?

a. Toad

b. Otter

c. Cat

d. Ghost

2) Hagrid named his dog Fuzzy?

a. True

b. False

3) Who was Alastor 'Mad-Eye' Moody flying with when he died?

a. Peter Pettigrew

b. Nymphadora Tonks

c. Horace Slughorn

d. Mundungus Fletcher

4) What spell is used to summon an object to you?

a. Accio

b. Papyrus Reparo

c. Expelliarmus

d. Lumos

5) In which prison did Gellert Grindelwald serve his sentence?

a. Dark Tower

b. Nurmengard

c. Azkaban

d. The Abandoned Substation

6) Hermione Granger's parents were dentists?

a. Yes

b. No

7) Can you use the Quaffle to score points in Quidditch?

a. No

b. Yes

8) The Imperius spell allows the wizard to control the actions of his opponent?

a. Yes

b. No

9) Draco Malfoy was able to kill Albus Dumbledore

a. False

b. True

10) Harry's training group, based in the Order of the Phoenix book, is called "Dumbledore's Attack"?

a. Yes

b. No

11) Whomping Willow grows in the Forbidden Forest?

a. Yes

b. No

12) Dumbledore has a scar that looks like a map of what?

a. The Area Of London

b. The East End

c. The London Underground

d. Hogsmeade

13) Who gave Potter The Firebolt broom?

a. Remus Lupin

b. Charles Weasley

c. Minerva McGonagall

d. Sirius Black

14) What country does Charlie Weasley work in?

a. Ukraine

b. Romania

c. Czechia

d. Moldova

15) Which country won first place in the Quidditch world Cup in the book "Goblet of Fire"?

a. Ireland

b. Bulgaria

c. Egypt

d. Wales

16) What does Hermione Granger's patronus look like?

a. Unicorn

b. Dog

c. Otter

d. Phoenix

17) Which horse-like creatures pull the school carriages at Hogwarts?

a. Pegasus

b. Niffler

c. Hippogriff

d. Thestrals

18) What potion did Potter win from Professor Slughorn?

a. Felix Felicis

b. Amortentia

c. Confusing Concoction

d. Pepperup Potion

19) What is Neville Longbottom most afraid of? Hint - think about the boggart.

a. Moon

b. Dragon

c. Gregory Goyle

d. Severus Snape

20) What was the name of the Goblin who first showed Harry his vault at Gringotts?

a. Dobby

b. Griphook

c. Winky

d. Gornuk

21) Whose wedding was attended by Potter in the movie "Harry Potter and the Deathly Hallows"?

a. Bill Weasley and Fleur Delacour

b. Remus Lupin and Nymphadora Tonks

c. Rolf Scamander and Luna Lovegood

d. Ronald Weasley and Hermione Granger

22) What is the name of the Ministry where Arthur Weasley works?

a. Improper Use of Magic Office

b. Department of Mysteries

c. Misuse of Muggle Artefacts

d. Office for the Detection and Confiscation of Counterfeit Defensive Spells and Protective Objects

23) What broom does Lucius Malfoy give the entire Slytherin Quidditch team?

a. Nimbus 2000

b. Nimbus 2001

c. Comet 260

d. Firebolt

24) What antidote saved Ron from being poisoned by Slughorn's mead?

a. Ashwinder eggs

b. Mandrake Restorative Draught

c. Bezoar

d. Sleeping Draught

25) What was the name of Tom Riddle's mother?

a. Merope Gaunt

b. Sybill Trelawney

c. Mary Elizabeth Cattermole

d. Arabella Doreen Figg

26) What name did Lupin and Tonks give their son?

a. Harry

b. Argus

c. Salazar

d. Teddy

27) What is the address of Sirius Black's family home?

a. 12 Grimmauld Place

b. 4 Privet Drive

c. 7 Spinner's End

d. 11 Ottery St Catchpole

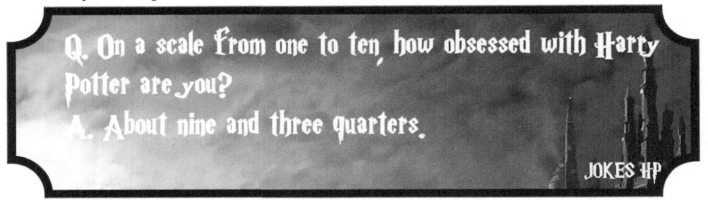

Q. On a scale from one to ten, how obsessed with Harry Potter are you?
A. About nine and three quarters.

JOKES HP

28) How many gifts did Dudley Dursley get on his eleventh birthday?

a. 11

b. 36

c. 12

d. 25

29) What animal could James Potter transfigure into?

a. Eagle

b. Stag

c. Dog

d. Cat

30) What does Hagrid call his dragon in the Philosopher's Stone?

a. Ginger

b. Norbert

c. Grawp

d. Peeves

LEVEL TWO ANSWERS

1. ➤ c) Cat

2. ➤ b) False

3. ➤ d) Mundungus Fletcher

4. ➤ a) Accio

5. ➤ b) Nurmengard

6. ➤ a) Yes

7. ➤ b) Yes

8. ➤ a) Yes

9. ➤ a) False

10. ➤ a) Yes

11. ➤ b) No

12. ➤ c) The London Underground

13. ➤ d) Sirius Black

14. ➤ b) Romania

15. ➤ a) Ireland

16. ➤ c) Otter

17. ➤ d) Thestrals

18. ➤ a) Felix Felicis

19. ➤ d) Severus Snape

20. ➤ b) Griphook

21. ➤ a) Bill Weasley and Fleur Delacour

22. ➤ c) Misuse of Muggle Artefacts

23. ➤ b) Nimbus 2001

24. ➤ c) Bezoar

25. ➤ a) Merope Gaunt

26. ➤ d) Teddy

27. ➤ a) 12 Grimmauld Place

28. ➤ b) 36

29. ➤ b) Stag

30. ➤ b) Norbert

Interesting Facts Part Two

• On Professor Dumbledore's left knee, there is a tattoo in the shape of the map of London Underground.

• Newt Scamander was closely related to a fellow student, Leta Lestrange. Leta Lestrange was also Bellatrix's relative.

• The majority of Block family members get their names from constellations or stars. Sirius is informally known as the "Dog Star." It reflects its distinction in its constellation, Canis Major, which means Greater Dog.

• Harry, Hermione, and Ron had Chocolate Frogs dedicated to them. And Ron, like Dumbledore, considers it the most significant achievement of his life.

• At first, Tom Felton read for the characters, Ron and Harry. But latër he was cast for the part Draco Malfoy.

TRIVIA LEVEL THREE. HARRY POTTER

1) Who is Draco Malfoy inviting to the Yule Ball in Goblet of Fire?

a. Pansy Parkinson

b. Millicent Bulstrode

c. Luna Lovegood

d. Marietta Edgecombe

2) What Animagus is Rita Skeeter?

a. A beetle

b. A dog

c. A lizard

d. An owl

3) Who said the phrase?: "Anything's possible if you've got enough nerve."

a. Albus Dumbledore

b. Cho Chang

c. Ginny Weasley

d. Sybill Trelawney

4) Who said the phrase?: "It is the quality of one's convictions that determines success, not the

number of followers?"

a. Filius Flitwick

b. Narcissa Malfoy

c. Igor Karkaroff

d. Remus Lupin

5) What is the model of the car that Ron and Harry flew in the book Chamber of Secrets?

a. Alfa Romeo Duetto

b. Ford Anglia

c. BMW 3 Series

d. Chevrolet Impala

6) Can I use a Mandrake draught against petrification?

a. Yes

b. No

7) Hagrid's mother was a giantess?

a. Yes

b. No

8) What was the name of Fleur Delacour's sister?

a. Gabrielle

b. Dolores

c. Molly

d. Isabelle

9) What do you call a person who is a muggle but has magical parents?

a. A muggle

b. A mudblood

c. A squib

10) The spell Sonorus increases the enemy's head?

a. Yes

b. No

11) Bill Weasley became a werewolf

a. True

b. False

12) One of the Deathly Hallows is the blood of a unicorn?

a. Yes

b. No

13) What position does Harry play on the Quidditch team?

a. Chaser

b. Beater

c. Keeper

d. Seeker

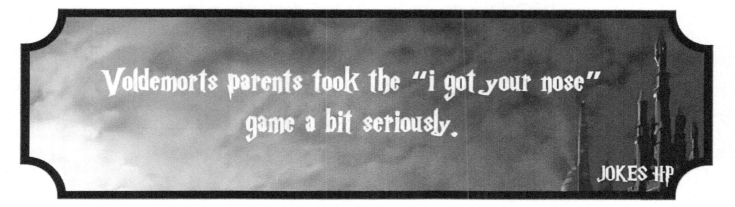

14) Which wizard Dumbledore defeat in 1945?

a. Gellert Grindelwald

b. Tom Marvolo Riddle

c. Nerida Vulchanova

d. Salazar Slytherin

15) What did Harry Potter trick Lucius Malfoy into giving Dobby?

a. A belt

b. A cane

c. A sock

d. White hair dye

16) What is the place where Harry godfather was?

a. Hogwarts

b. Forbidden Forest

c. Durmstrang Institute

d. Azakaban prison

17) What insects is Ron very afraid of?

a. Ant

b. Bug

c. Spider

d. Cockroach

18) What is the name of Dumbledore's Phoenix?

a. Tenebrus

b. Hermes

c. Fawkes

d. Maestro

19) What is the name of the Slytherin Quidditch Captain?

a. Marcus Flint

b. Cedric Diggory

c. Dean Thomas

d. Oliver Wood

20) What the name of the tournament in Harry Potter and the Goblet of Fire?

a. Triwizard Tournament

b. Yule Ball

c. Battle of the three wizards

d. Order of the Phoenix

21) In whose guise does Harry attack Ron's father in a dream?

a. Peter Pettigrew

b. A Boggart

c. A deer

d. A snake

22) Who's Peeeves?

a. A centaur

b. A poltertgeist

c. A goblins

d. A triturus

23) What house did the Sorting Hat almost put Harry Potter in?

a. Ravenclaw

b. Hufflepuff

c. Slytherin

d. Other school

24) What type of wizard is Harry's godfather?

a. Animagus

b. Muggle

c. Werewolf

d. Metamorphmagus

25) What magical plant that make Harry Potter use to make him still breth underwater in Goblet

of Fire?

a. Asphodel

b. Gillyweed

c. Valerian

d. Lovage

26) What kind of ice cream did Harry Potter get at the zoo?

a. Lemon Ice Pop

b. Mint Ice Pop

c. Butter Pecan ice cream

d. Neapolitan ice cream

27) What was the name of Percy Weasley's owl?

a. Errol

b. Pigwidgeon

c. Brodwin

d. Hermes

28) What village was Harry Potter born in?

a. Barnton

b. Montrose

c. Godric's Hollow

d. Hogsmeade

29) What color are Potter's eyes?

a. Light-blue

b. Green

c. Gray

d. Brown

30) Who was the secret keeper in the Potter family?

a. Peter Pettigrew

b. Sirius Black

c. Severus Snape

LEVEL THREE ANSWERS

1. ➤ a) Pansy Parkinson

2. ➤ a) A beetle

3. ➤ c) Ginny Weasley

4. ➤ d) Remus Lupin

5. ➤ b) Ford Anglia

6. ➤ a) Yes

7. ➤ a) Yes

8. ➤ a) Gabrielle

9. ➤ c) A squib

10. ➤ b) No

11. ➤ b) False

12. ➤ b) No

13. ➤ d) Seeker

14. ➤ a) Gellert Grindelwald

15. ➤ c) A sock

16. ➤ d) Azakaban prison

17. ➤ c) Spider

18. ➤ c) Fawkes

19. ➤ a) Marcus Flint

20. ➤ a) Triwizard Tournament

21. ➤ d) A snake

22. ➤ b) A poltertgeist

23. ➢ c) Slytherin

24. ➢ a) Animagus

25. ➢ b) Gillyweed

26. ➢ a) Lemon Ice Pop

27. ➢ d) Hermes

28. ➢ c) Godric's Hollow

29. ➢ b) Green

30. ➢ a) Peter Pettigrew

Interesting Facts Part Three

• Muggles, non-magic people, are called "No-Maj" in America.

• In Latin, "Expecto Patronum" means "I await a guardian."

• Draco Malfoy would have schooled at the Durmstrang Institute if his father had decided. But his mother didn't want him to be too far from home.

• Professor Snape character is based mainly On J.K. Rowling's old chemistry teacher.

TRIVIA LEVEL FOUR. REMUS LUPIN

1) How many times does Filch make Ron polish all the Quidditch cups?

a. 7

b. 8

c. 14

d. 15

2) Who gave Harry the nimbus 2000?

a. Sirius Black

b. Remus Lupin

c. Rubeus Hagrid

d. Minerva McGonagall

3) What did Hermionie give Harry for his birthday in Harry Potter and the Prisoner of Azkaban?

a. A Broomstick Servicing Kit.

b. Set of books.

c. Jacket

d. Time-Turner

4) With whom Harry had your first kiss?

a. Arabella Doreen Figg

b. Lavender Brown

c. Katie Bell

d. Cho Chang

5) Where did Harry Potter first met Professor Quirinus Quirrell?

a. The Leaky Cauldron

b. Hogwarts Express

c. Privet Drive

d. Weasleys' Wizard Wheeses

6) Where did Harry first speak to the snake?

a. Hogwarts

b. Magical Menagerie

c. At The Zoo

d. Godric's Hollow

7) What toy was Harry playing with in his closet under the stairs?

a. Toy Soldiers

b. Magic wand

c. Toy car

d. Sword

8) What did the boggart turn into for Ron?

a. Howler

b. Giant spider

c. Snake

d. Library

9) What did the boggart turn into for Harry?

a. Lord Voldemort

b. Severus Snape

c. Giant dog

d. Dementors

COLOR
ME

10) Spell to get rid of a baggart?

a. Finestra

b. Ridikulus

c. Expelliarmus

d. Confundo

11) Who was Harry's first quidditch match was against?

a. Hufflepuff

b. Chudley Cannons

c. Ravenclaw

d. Slytherin

12) In what mirror did Harry see his parents?

a. The Mirror Of Erised

b. Two-way mirror

c. Penelope Clearwater's mirror

d. Foe-Glass

13) Who was Harry's first Quidditch captain?

a. Cedric Diggory

b. Oliver Wood

c. Katie Bell

d. Marcus Flint

Q: How did Aragog get in touch with other spiders?
A: The world wide WEB

JOKES HP

14) What did grandma give Neville in his first year at Hogwarts?

a. Remembrall

b. Dissimulator

c. Dragon claw

d. Mimbulus mimbletonia

15) How many Seekers are on a Quidditch team?

a. Two

b. Three

c. Four

d. One

16) Who created the philosopher's stone?

a. Gellert Grindelwald

b. Nicolas Flamel

c. Isolt Sayre

d. Godric Gryffindor

17) What is Ron Weasley's Quidditch number?

a. #9

b. #7

c. #2

d. #0

18) What quidditch team did Ron support?

a. Holyhead Harpies

b. Pride of Portree

c. Chudley Cannons

d. Appleby Arrows

19) What are offensive players on a Quidditch team called?

a. Chasers

b. Beater

c. Seeker

d. Keeper

20) Which quidditch team did Oliver Wood become reserve keeper for?

a. Woollongong Warriors

b. Gimbi Giant

c. Grodzisk Goblins

d. Puddlemere United

21) Who was the captain of the Gryffindor Quidditch team in Harry Potter and the order of the Phoenix?

a. Katie Bell

b. Angelina Weasley

c. Romilda Vane

d. Lavender Brown

22) Who taught Harry defense against the dark arts in his second year?

a. Gilderoy Lockhart

b. Griphook

c. Quirinus Quirrell

d. Bartemius Crouch Junior

23) Who has heard even half of the prophecy about Harry and the Dark Lord?

a. Gornuk

b. Frank Longbottom

c. Severus Snape

d. Horace Slughorn

24) Who was a direct descendant of Lord Voldemort's mother?

a. Gideon Flatworthy

b. Rowena Ravenclaw

c. Gellert Grindelwald

d. Salazar Slytherin

25) Where did Voldemort work after he left Hogwarts?

a. Gregorovitch Zauberstäbe

b. Borgin and Burkes

c. Flourish and Blotts

d. Ye Olde Curiosity Shop

26) Who always carried a camera while studying at Hogwarts?

a. Michael Corner

b. Marietta Edgecombe

c. Colin Creevey

d. Terry Boot

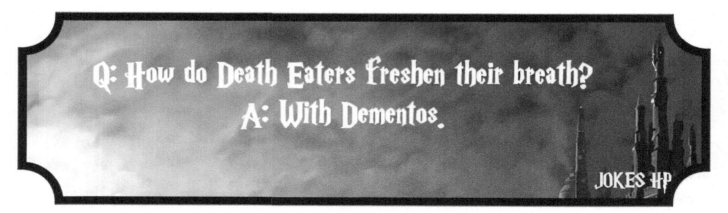

27) Who was the headmaster of Hogwarts when Tom Riddle was there?

a. Armando Dippet

b. Phineas Nigellus Black

c. Elizabeth Burke

d. Basil Fronsac

28) Who told Voldemort where The Lost Diadem was?

a. Rowena Ravenclaw

b. Helena Ravenclaw

c. Violetta Black

d. Caractacus Burke

29) Who did the Dark Lord steal the Hufflepuff Cup and Slytherin medallion from?

a. Helga Hufflepuff

b. Hepzibah Smith

c. Zacharias Smith

d. Borgin

30) In what year was the Secret Room first opened?

a. 1943

b. 1945

c. 1998

d. 1996

LEVEL FOUR ANSWERS

1. ➢ c) 14

2. ➢ d) Minerva McGonagall

3. ➢ a) A Broomstick Servicing Kit.

4. ➢ d) Cho Chang

5. ➢ a) The Leaky Cauldron

6. ➢ c) At The Zoo

7. ➢ a) Toy Soldiers

8. ➢ b) Giant spider

9. ➢ d) Dementors

10. ➢ b) Ridikulus

11. ➢ d) Slytherin

12. ➢ a) The Mirror Of Erised

13. ➢ b) Oliver Wood

14. ➢ a) Remembrall

15. ➢ d) One

16. ➢ b) Nicolas Flamel

17. ➢ c) #2

18. ➢ c) Chudley Cannons

19. ➢ a) Chasers

20. ➢ d) Puddlemere United

21. ➢ b) Angelina Weasley

22. ➢ a) Gilderoy Lockhart

23. ➢ c) Severus Snape

24. ➢ d) Salazar Slytherin

25. ➢ b) Borgin and Burkes

26. ➢ c) Colin Creevey

27. ➢ a) Armando Dippet

28. ➢ b) Helena Ravenclaw

29. ➢ b) Hepzibah Smith

30. ➢ a) 1943

Interesting Facts Part Four

• In Europe only, Quidditch is the commonest sport amongst wizards and witches. However, people in America preferred the game Quodpot.

• Ginny Weasley came to be an expert in playing Quidditch after Hogwarts. Then after having her first son with Harry, he became part of the Daily Prophet's sports editorial staff.

• Ron's Patronus was a Jack Russell Terrier, while that of Hermione was an otter. Jack Russell Terriers are known for chasing otters.

• Readers of Harry Potter found it difficult pronouncing Hermione's name. so Rowling created a scene where she explained her name to Viktor Krum.

1) What kind of monster lives in the Chamber of Secrets?

a. Dragon

b. Ogre

c. Acromantula

d. Basilisk

2) Who did the Basilisk kill?

a. Moaning Myrtle

b. Morfin Gaunt

c. Sir Cadogan

d. Cedric Diggory

3) What is the name of Hagrid's Acromantula?

a. Norbert

b. Fluffy

c. Aragog

d. Mosague

4) Who are these corpses that follow the Dark wizard's orders?

a. Banshee

b. Vampire

c. Inferi

d. Kappa

5) How the North American School of Witchcraft and Wizardry is known as?

a. Ilvermorny

b. Durmstrang

c. Castelobruxo

d. Beauxbatons

6) Who is the half-blood Prince?

a. Albus Dumbledore

b. Severus Snape

c. Quirinus Quirrell

d. Horace Slughorn

7) What is the name of Albus Dumbledore's sister?

a. Anna

b. Ariana

c. Ioanna

d. Violetta

8) Which ear did George Weasley lose?

a. Left

b. Right

9) How much does one Galleon cost?

a. 100 Sickles

b. 10 Sickles

c. 17 Sickles

d. 15 Sickles

10) What Felix Felicis do?

a. Makes the victim sneeze

b. Gives ability to change your voice

c. Gives an antidote

d. Gives good luck

11) Who has bewitched bludger?

a. Dobby

b. Severus Snape

c. Quirinus Quirrell

d. Lucius Malfoy

12) What is Cho Chang's position on the Ravenclaw Quidditch team?

a. Chasers

b. Seeker

c. Beater

d. Keeper

13) What spells did the half-blood Prince invent?

a. Levicorpus

b. Colloportus

c. Sectumsempra

d. Serpensortia

14) After meeting a Dementor, what kind of thing will make a person happy?

a. Bertie Bott's Every Flavour Beans

b. Coconut Ice

c. Pumpkin fizz

d. Chocolate

15) What is Umbridge's favorite color?

a. Red

b. Turquoise

c. Mauve

d. Pink

16) What does Harry Potter use to kill the Basilisk?

a. Spell

b. Potion

c. Sword of Gryffindor

d. Deathly Hallows

17) Which of them is not one of Albus Dumbledore's middle names?

a. Percival

b. Augustine

c. Wulfric

d. Brian

18) How fast can a Firebolt fly from 0-150 mph?

a. 11 seconds

b. 10 seconds

c. 12 seconds

d. 15 seconds

19) What wood is Ron's first wand made of?

a. Ash

b. Mahogany

c. Baobab

d. Asp

20) Which dragon will Viktor Krum face in the first task of the Triwizard Tournament?

a. Ukrainian Ironbelly

b. Hebridean Black

c. Chinese Fireball

d. Hungarian Horntail

21) Nymphadora Tonks was a Gryffindor student

a. False

b. True

22) For 1 Sickle there are 27 Knuts

a. False

b. True

23) JK Rowling's last name rhymes with bowling

a. False

b. True

24) Hermione got all the " honours" in her O.W.L. exams.

a. False

b. True

25) What is the name of the class that students must enter through the hatch?

a. Transfiguration

b. Charms

c. History of Magic

d. Divination

26) What is Hermione Granger's middle name?

a. Jean

b. Vivian

c. Jane

d. Eda

27) Romilda Vane put a love potion in Harry's chocolate frogs

a. False

b. True

28) What's the name of aunt Marge's dog?

a. Fang

b. Ripper

c. Fluffy

d. Sam

29) What potion will make the drinker tell the truth?

a. Amortentia

b. Volubilis Potion

c. Veritasearumm

30) Who commands the Headless Hunt?

a. Cuthbert Binns

b. Bloody Baron

c. Sir Nicholas de Mimsy-Porpington

d. Patrick Delaney-Podmore

LEVEL FIVE ANSWERS

1. ➤ d) Basilisk

2. ➤ a) Moaning Myrtle

3. ➤ c) Aragog

4. ➤ c) Inferi

5. ➤ a) Ilvermorny

6. ➤ b) Severus Snape

7. ➤ b) Ariana

8. ➤ a) Left

9. ➤ c) 17 Sickles

10. ➤ d) Gives good luck

11. ➤ a) Dobby

12. ➤ b) Seeker

13. ➤ c) Sectumsempra; a) Levicorpus

14. ➤ d) Chocolate

15. ➤ d) Pink

16. ➤ c) Sword of Gryffindor

17. ➤ b) Augustine

18. ➤ b) 10 seconds

19. ➤ a) Ash

20. ➤ c) Chinese Fireball

21. ➤ a) False

22. ➤ a) False

23. ➤ b) True

24. ➤ a) False

25. ➤ d) Divination

26. ➤ a) Jean

27. ➤ a) False

28. ➤ b) Ripper

29. ➤ c) Veritasearumm

30. ➤ d) Patrick Delaney-Podmore

Interesting Facts Part Five

• Fred Weasly and George's birthday is on the 1st of April.

• Just as you know, Dementors are deadly magical creatures. According to Rowling, they were a representation of depression and were based on her experience with it. Chocolate was used to neutralize the effects of a Dementor.

• When Michael Jackson offered to produce a Harry Potter musical with J. K. Rowling, she rejected it.

• Rupert Grint had to be taken out of the set in the Horcrux kissing scene with Hermione and Harry. He just couldn't hold back his giggles.

• George couldn't get himself back together after Fred died. He also was never able to create a Patronus again.

TRIVIA LEVEL SIX. HERMIONE GRANGER

Note: Further 2 levels become more and more complex and will not have any answer options. Write your answers in Notepad or in the fields marked below.

1) What does Luna Lovegood's father do for a living?

Player 1 _____

Player 2 _____

Player 3 _____

Player 4 _____

2) What is Albus Dumbledore's full name?

Player 1 _____
Player 2 _____
Player 3 _____
Player 4 _____

3) What is the name of the first Harry Potter book?

Player 1 _____

Player 2 _____

Player 3 _____

Player 4 _____

4) What are the names of Ron's mother and father?

Player 1 _____

Player 2 _____

Player 3 _____

Player 4 _____

5) How does Harry Potter catch his very first Snitch?

Player 1 _____

Player 2 _____

Player 3 _____

Player 4 _____

6) What is the name of the person who runs the flight classes?

Player 1 _____

Player 2 _____

Player 3 _____

Player 4 _____

7) What is the name of the newspaper that appears in 7 books?

Player 1 _____

Player 2 _____

Player 3 _____

Player 4 _____

8) Who killed Bella Lestrange?

Player 1 _____

Player 2 _____

Player 3 _____

Player 4 _____

9) What is Dumbledore's brother's name?

Player 1 _____

Player 2 _____

Player 3 _____

Player 4 _____

10) And who is Fluffy?

Player 1 _____

Player 2 _____

Player 3 _____

Player 4 _____

11) Who became Prime Minister of Magic after Cornelius Fudge?

Player 1 _____

Player 2 _____

Player 3 _____

Player 4 _____

12) What is the name of the Hogwarts muggle studies teacher that Voldemort killed?

Player 1 _____

Player 2 _____

Player 3 _____

Player 4 _____

13) Who is the hogwarts librarian?

Player 1 _____

Player 2 _____

Player 3 _____

Player 4 _____

> Q. Why Can't Harry Potter Tell Apart His Potions Pot And His Best Mate?
> A. Because They're Both Cauldron.
>
> JOKES HP

14) Where is Hogwarts library?

Player 1 _____

Player 2 _____

Player 3 _____

Player 4 _____

15) How much do you have to pay for a ticket on the Knight Bus if it comes with hot chocolate?

Player 1 _____

Player 2 _____

Player 3 _____

Player 4 _____

16) Who was Hermione portraying with Polyjuice Potion in the Ministry in The deathly Hallows?

Player 1 _____

Player 2 _____

Player 3 _____

Player 4 _____

17) Where does Vernon Dursley work?

Player 1 _____

Player 2 _____

Player 3 _____

Player 4 _____

18) What can I see on the Marauder's map?

Player 1 _____

Player 2 _____

Player 3 _____

Player 4 _____

19) Why was this huge Whomping Willow tree planted?

Player 1 _____

Player 2 _____

Player 3 _____

Player 4 _____

20) How affectionately did Lavender Brown call Ron?

Player 1 _____

Player 2 _____

Player 3 _____

Player 4 _____

21) Who did Hermione Granger take to Slughorn's Christmas Party?

Player 1 _____

Player 2 _____

Player 3 _____

Player 4 _____

22) What pet does Hermione Granger have and what is it called?

Player 1 _____

Player 2 _____

Player 3 _____

Player 4 _____

23) What spell does Hermione use on Harry when they are captured?

Player 1 _____

Player 2 _____

Player 3 _____

Player 4 _____

24) Who does Sirius want to kill now that he is out of Azkaban?

Player 1 _____

Player 2 _____

Player 3 _____

Player 4 _____

25) Where did Ron and his family just return from before returning to school for year 3?

Player 1 _____

Player 2 _____

Player 3 _____

Player 4 _____

26) Who was the first person to ever create a horcrux?

Player 1 _____

Player 2 _____

Player 3 _____

Player 4 _____

27) What was the date of Voldemort's death?

Player 1 _____

Player 2 _____

Player 3 _____

Player 4 _____

28) How many balls are there in Quidditch?

Player 1 _____

Player 2 _____

Player 3 _____

Player 4 _____

29) Why did Voldemort try to kill Harry when he was very young?

Player 1 _____

Player 2 _____

Player 3 _____

Player 4 _____

30) What was Winky the house-elf afraid of?

Player 1 _____

Player 2 _____

Player 3 _____

Player 4 _____

LEVEL SIX ANSWERS

1. ➤ Works for Quibbler

2. ➤ Albus Percival Wulfric Brian Dumbledore

3. ➤ Harry Potter and the Philosopher's Stone

4. ➤ Arthur and Molly Weasley

5. ➤ Harry caught the Snitch in his mouth

6. ➤ Madam Rolanda Hooch

7. ➤ Daily Prophet

8. ➤ Molly Weasley

9. ➤ Aberforth

10. ➤ Three-headed dog

11. ➤ Rufus Scrimgeour

12. ➤ Charity Burbage

13. ➤ Irma Pince

14. ➤ On the third floor of the castle

15. ➤ 14 sickles

16. ➤ Mafalda Hopkirk

17. ➤ Grunnings – A drill manufacturer

18. ➤ The location of everyone at Hogwarts

19. ➤ To protect Remus Lupin

20. ➤ Won-Won

21. ➤ Cormac McLaggen

22. ➤ Crookshanks was Hermione Granger's pet cat. He was half-Kneazle.

23. ➤ Stinging Jinx

24. ➤ Ron's rat

25. ➤ Egypt

26. ➤ Herpo The Fowl

27. ➤ 2nd May

28. ➤ 4

29. ➤ Because of a prophecy that was overheard by one of Voldemort's Deatheaters

30. ➤ Heights

Interesting Facts Part Six

• Hermione, after Hogwarts, worked in the Department for the Regulation and Control of Magical Creatures. Working for the Ministry of Magic helped her to gain rights for magical creatures like house elves. Then, she switched to the Magical Law Enforcement Department.

• Ron and Harry became Aurors and changed the Department entirely.

• Harry became the leader of the Auror very quickly, before heading the Department of Magical Law Enforcement. Often, at Hog warts, he also lectured people on Defense Against the Dark Arts.

• Ginny and Harry's children were named after Harry's parents, James and Lily. Then, Albus Dumbledore, Sirius Black, Luna Lovegood, and Severus Snape.

• Rowling probably made Hermione resemble her. They even shared the same favorite animal, an otter, as a Patronus.

TRIVIA LEVEL SEVEN. ALBUS DUMBLEDORE

1) Who's Peeves?

Player 1 _____

Player 2 _____

Player 3 _____

Player 4 _____

2) What spell is used to summon the dark mark?

Player 1 _____

Player 2 _____

Player 3 _____

Player 4 _____

3) What's the name of Ollivander's?

Player 1 _____

Player 2 _____

Player 3 _____

Player 4 _____

4) Who taught the Care of Magical Creatures before Hagrid?

Player 1 _____

Player 2 _____

Player 3 _____

Player 4 _____

5) Who was born first - Fred or George Weasley?

Player 1 _____

Player 2 _____

Player 3 _____

Player 4 _____

6) Who teased Moaning Myrtle about her glasses?

Player 1 _____

Player 2 _____

Player 3 _____

Player 4 _____

7) What is the name of Nicholas Flamel's wife?

Player 1 _____

Player 2 _____

Player 3 _____

Player 4 _____

8) What state gives Tonks the ability to transform their features?

Player 1 _____

Player 2 _____

Player 3 _____

Player 4 _____

9) What do Bill and Fleur call their daughter?

Player 1 _____

Player 2 _____

Player 3 _____

Player 4 _____

e Peverell brothers

_____

_____

Player 3 _____

Player 4 _____

11) How many stairs are there in Hogwarts castle?

Player 1 _____

Player 2 _____

Player 3 _____

Player 4 _____

12) What number does Mr Weasley dial to get into the ministry?

Player 1 _____

Player 2 _____

Player 3 _____

Player 4 _____

13) What kind of power the Dementors have on people?

Player 1 _____

Player 2 _____

Player 3 _____

Player 4 _____

14) Who's Group?

Player 1 _____

Player 2 _____

Player 3 _____

Player 4 _____

15) What magical talent does Harry share with Voldemort?

Player 1 _____

Player 2 _____

Player 3 _____

Player 4 _____

16) How did the Phoenix save Harry?

Player 1 _____

Player 2 _____

Player 3 _____

Player 4 _____

17) What made Dumbledore's hand turn shrivel and black?

Player 1 _____

Player 2 _____

Player 3 _____

Player 4 _____

18) What does Slughorn want from Aragog after his death?

Player 1 _____

Player 2 _____

Player 3 _____

Player 4 _____

19) What wand is buried with Dumbledore?

Player 1 _____

Player 2 _____

Player 3 _____

Player 4 _____

20) Why is Snape protecting Harry?

Player 1 _____

Player 2 _____

Player 3 _____

Player 4 _____

21) In which candy does Harry find Dumbledore's card?

Player 1 _____

Player 2 _____

_____

_____

first of Dumbledore's duel with Grindelwald?

Player 1 _____

Player 2 _____

Player 3 _____

Player 4 _____

23) Which newspaper tried to discredit Dumbledore in Harry Potter and the order of the Phoenix?

Player 1 _____

Player 2 _____

Player 3 _____

Player 4 _____

24) Dumbledore's first job at Hogwarts was teaching what subject?

Player 1 _____

Player 2 _____

Player 3 _____

Player 4 _____

25) What house did Dumbledore study in?

Player 1 _____

Player 2 _____

Player 3 _____

Player 4 _____

26) What other pseudonym was JK Rowling published under?

Player 1 _____

Player 2 _____

Player 3 _____

Player 4 _____

i don't get how people can say harry potter is fake.
like just watch
the movies they literally caught everything on film.

JOKES HP

27) At the end of Harry Potter and the Sorcerer's Stone, why does Dumbledore award Ron fifty points for Gryffindor?

Player 1 _____

Player 2 _____

Player 3 _____

Player 4 _____

28) Who said this? "I was lucky enough not to be arrested actually"

Player 1 _____

Player 2 _____

Player 3 _____

Player 4 _____

29) What does Ron receive from his mother after crashing the family car?

Player 1 _____

Player 2 _____

Player 3 _____

Player 4 _____

30) Where was Dumbledore buried?

Player 1 _____

Player 2 _____

Player 3 _____

Player 4 _____

LEVEL SEVEN ANSWERS

1. ➢ A Poltergeist

2. ➢ Morsmodre

3. ➢ Garrick

4. ➢ Silvanus Kettleburn

5. ➢ Fred

6. ➢ Olive Hornby

7. ➢ Perenelle

8. ➢ She's a Metamorphmagus

9. ➢ Victoire

10. ➢ Cadmus, Antioch and Ignotus

11. ➢ 142

12. ➢ 62442

13. ➢ They drain them of all happiness

14. ➢ Hagrid's half brother

15. ➢ He's a Parselmouth

16. ➢ His tears

17. ➢ Marvolo Gaunt's ring

18. ➢ His venom

19. ➢ The Elder Wand

20. ➢ Snape had loved Lily since they were children

21. ➢ Chocolate Frogs

22. ➢ His sister

23. ➢ Daily Prophet

24. ➢ Transfiguration

25. ➢ Gryffindor

26. ➢ Robert Galbraith

27. ➢ Game of chess

28. ➢ Serious Black

29. ➢ Howler

30. ➢ Lake at Hogwarts

Interesting Facts Part Seven

• Arthur Weasley enters the number 6-2-4-4-2 in the phone booth to reach the Ministry of magic with Harry. On a regular telephone, the letters under those numbers read "magic."

• Dumbledore was already 115 years old when Snape killed him.

• Voldemort was aged 71 when he died in the Battle of Hogwarts.

• Ernie and Stanley, the Knight Bus' driver and conductor, shared the same names with Rowling's grandfathers.

• At first, Lupin was not supposed to die. But having a child lose a parent is one of the worst things about war. So Rowling had to add that part too.

Dear Readers!

Thank You for Purchasing & Reading! I hope this can help y'all to love the Harry Potter Universe, as much as I do! Enjoy!

If you leave without writing a review about the guide, one sad author will become more... :)

Made in the USA
Monee, IL
26 January 2022

89900731R00118